Made with Love

Delectable Donuts (page 154)

appetite
by RANDOM HOUSE

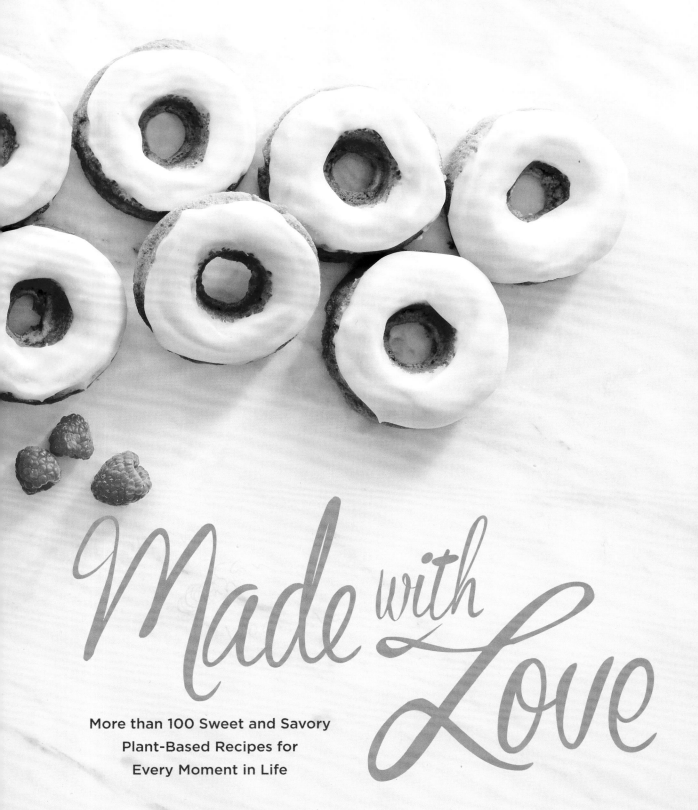

Made with Love

More than 100 Sweet and Savory
Plant-Based Recipes for
Every Moment in Life

Kelly Childs and Erinn Weatherbie

Appetite by Random House® and colophon are registered trademarks of Penguin Random House LLC.

Kelly's Bake Shoppe® is a registered trademark of Kelly's Bake Shoppe Inc.
Lettuce Love Café® is a registered trademark of Lettuce Love Café Inc.
Are You Living Your Life Yet?® is a registered trademark of Childs and Weatherbie Inc.

Library and Archives Canada Cataloguing in Publication is available upon request

ISBN: 978-0-147-52983-1
eBook ISBN: 978-0-147-52984-8

Cover and book photography: Alyssa Wodabek and Chris Sue-Chu
Printed and bound in China

Published in Canada by Appetite by Random House®,
a division of Penguin Random House Canada Limited

www.penguinrandomhouse.ca

10   9   8   7   6   5   4   3   2   1

appetite   Penguin
by RANDOM HOUSE   Random
House

This book is dedicated to my dad.

It is only fitting because he deserves the credit more than anyone else.

I know I would not be here without the creative dreaming and magical values he instilled in me.

For you, Dad. Thank you for the magic. (Wink-wink.)

Kelly

To Kindfood: thank you for giving us the inspiration, strength, love and passion to create

Kelly's Bake Shoppe and Lettuce Love Café. You will forever be in our hearts.

Erinn

Chocolate Cupcakes (page 142)

Contents

Savory Moments

Bake Shoppe Treats!

The Bakery Is Magic

"Once upon a time there was a little girl who loved baking mud pies. She loved it so much she created her own imaginary bakery. As she grew up so did her baking. Now she has a beautiful daughter, who has followed in her footsteps . . ."

L.O.V.E. It's the first word I learned to spell and it's the word that conjures up my life, and our Bake Shoppe, in a nutshell. Starting the Bake Shoppe wasn't something that I set out to do, it wasn't my goal. But when I think back on my childhood it seems like it was inevitable.

My sister, Shannon, and I had a special, magical childhood. Our father, Russ Childs, was uniquely artistic, creative, imaginative, loving and very generous. On Christmas morning, there were Santa's muddy boot prints (they could only have been Santa's) and reindeer footprints (Rudolph's!) tracked in the snow outside our windows. The house would be lavishly decorated with lights, candles, garlands, tinsel and candy, a wonderland like something Dickens would have imagined.

With my dad, we didn't just cut flowers from our backyard and give them to my mom for her to put in a vase: we had flower-arranging lessons on a massive table, complete with vases, scissors, rulers and Dad teaching us the basics of design!

But the ultimate thrill for me was the outdoor kitchen and bakery Dad created for us in the backyard ravine, complete with cake pans, cookie sheets, cutlery, muffin pans, a roaster and even a rotary eggbeater. All of these were hand-me-downs from my mom, but the kitchen was Dad's idea, and it was pure magic to me. My love of making dirt cakes and mud pies in our backyard was the catalyst for Kelly's Bake Shoppe. What I experienced as a child—innocence, fun, creative passion and everyday celebration—is what we now try to share with everyone who walks through the doors at the bakery, and it's what we hope to share with this book, too.

My father was my inspiration, my mentor and my biggest fan. He encouraged me to dream big and believe in myself. My dad died suddenly in 1995, when I was 32 and he was

just 61. My daughter, Erinn, was five when he died and she was his very special golden girl. They spent hours together laughing, dreaming, and painting, coloring and drawing make-believe stories. He always said she had a beautifully shaped head, full of remarkable brains, and that she would be a superstar. Well, she is, Dad!

Erinn and I dreamed up every detail of Kelly's Bake Shoppe together, and now we get to spend every day there, side by side, as the mom-and-daughter team making the magic happen. What thrills us more than anything is when we see the ecstatic faces of kids and adults alike enjoying the treats we baked just for them; it's their joy that transports me back to *my* magical childhood.

At Kelly's Bake Shoppe, we are the healthier bakery; we make and serve treats that are gluten-free, dairy-free, egg-free and peanut-free, all made with plant-based, natural, organic ingredients. We want to include everyone in the delicious fun, so that people with allergies, food intolerances or restricted diets can all indulge. Because everyone deserves the happiness of a treat, or a little magical escape from their busy lives, at least for the time it takes to eat a cupcake. As it says outside our Bake Shoppe, "You can't buy happiness but you can buy cupcakes, and that's kind of the same thing."

Made with love, and magic,

Kelly xo

Our Story

Before there was Kelly's Bake Shoppe, there was Lettuce Love Café, and before there was Lettuce Love, there was Kindfood. Kindfood started it all. Well, a family road trip to a farm sanctuary in 2008 really started it all.

We set off for Farm Sanctuary in Watkins Glen, New York, completely unaware of the life-changing experience it would turn out to be. We packed Ken (Kelly's husband) and Mike (Erinn's boyfriend) into the car with us and drove to visit this peaceful retreat for rescued farm animals. At the sanctuary we learned for the first time about the full extent of factory farming, big agriculture and about what animals have to endure in the process. We came to truly understand the suffering that humans inflict upon billions of animals a year in the name of mass-produced "food." It was such a moving experience that on the way home, as we reflected on what we had learned, we decided that somehow we had to make a difference in the world.

At the same time, although she had long lived a very healthy lifestyle, Kelly was experiencing some serious health issues and was reading more and more about the health benefits of moving to an exclusively plant-based diet (more about this on page 6). Over the next several months, as our knowledge about plant-based eating grew, so did our passion for living cleanly and kindly, and our desire to help others to do the same. Then one day, during a vacation with Ken, the idea for Kindfood—a place to show people how easy plant-based eating could be—came suddenly to Kelly's mind. Kindfood would be a café, bakery and grocery store, and a way to help people realize that you can change your life through consuming food that is kind to your body, kind to the planet and kind to the animals: Kindfood. This would be our way of executing change in the world!

Just a couple of months later a For Lease sign went up on a little shop around the corner from our home in Burlington, Ontario. It was so quaint and perfect that we knew we had found the perfect home for Kindfood to grow.

KINDFOOD

We opened our doors in May 2010, as a café, bakery and grocery store, with a juice and smoothie bar, too. Kindfood was an instant hit, and we were so busy that we were soon tripping over each other in this 1,000-square-foot space. By January of the next year we realized that what people *really* wanted was our homemade food, not the groceries and produce they could buy elsewhere.

We stopped selling groceries and renovated the business into a 25-seat café and bakery. It was great! In six months' time, we had more than 5,000 fans on Facebook! Kelly was there every day, and both Erinn and Mike were dedicating all of their time between university and college classes. We all worked our socks off to keep up with the demand.

Business was going really well, but both the savory (café component) and the sweet (bakery side) were doing so well that soon there wasn't room for both of them. On Saturday mornings, doing the bakery bake—using every horizontal workspace and counter imaginable—did not allow for the café to get prepped for its day. It was a daily battle over space, and we even went so far as to renovate again to reconfigure the kitchen, but it was only delaying the inevitable: we needed more space. It was time for us to take the bakery out on its own, just us girls.

KELLY'S BAKE SHOPPE IS BORN!

We signed the lease for Kelly's Bake Shoppe in May of 2012. We would very soon no longer have to smell the lovely aroma of onions and garlic (with onion tears running down our cheeks) while baking cupcakes and brownies. We knew then that our baking was making people happy and we were committed to making the Bake Shoppe a success.

Fast forward through six months of renovations, four declined bank loans, three accepted bank loans, a 12-man construction crew (of course Ken was the Lead Handyman Extraordinaire and our personal entrepreneur coach), the training of a whole new tribe of staff, the developement of new and updated recipes (scaled out tenfold), not to mention the addition of a beautiful new picture window . . . and Kelly's Bake Shoppe opened in December 2012.

We hit the ground running with incredible support on social media, our kind and incredibly personable staff and sweet treats that would soon become internationally-recognized and award-winning. Kelly's Bake Shoppe, something this mom and daughter had birthed together, was born. As a mom-and-daughter team we complement each other in ways we had no idea we were capable of doing, and yet here we are: the yin-and-yang entrepreneur team.

KINDFOOD BECOMES LETTUCE LOVE

But our renovations didn't stop there. We thought for a brief time that we would be able to relax into our new digs at the Bake Shoppe and relish the fruits of our labor once the doors opened. Finally we would have some well-deserved *coasting* time. What were we thinking?!

Out of nowhere, Kindfood was served a "cease and desist" letter from a U.S. trademark law firm that represented a company that shared our name. They were big players and decided to descend on our little Kindfood in Burlington, Ontario, to enforce their trademark and stop us using the name. We had to learn a great deal, very fast, about how to defend our family business. Then, after carefully weighing out the pros and cons, we finally, with sobbing tears, decided to say goodbye to the name Kindfood. It was one of the hardest decisions we have ever had to make. Kindfood was created with the deepest of love, and with a loyalty and commitment to change the world. We had thousands of followers and we were so afraid that we would lose our recognition of who we were.

But there was no time to wallow. We needed a new name, and fast. So Kelly locked herself on the second floor of the bakery and sat quietly to allow the thoughts to flow. She knew the word "love" would be a part of it, but it was only when she truly forgave the loss of the name Kindfood that Lettuce Love (a play on "let us love") came into her mind like a freight train. We gave Kindfood a loving burial and Lettuce Love Café opened in December 2013, even busier than before! Today Lettuce Love is run by Mike, while we focus on doing what we do best: making the magic happen at Kelly's Bake Shoppe.

INSIDE THE BAKE SHOPPE

Upon entering Kelly's Bake Shoppe you can't help but feel the warm, positive energy. The sound of music in the air, the natural wood floors and the vanilla cream–colored walls envelop you in an organically natural setting. Our custom bookshelves hold the Bake Shoppe's pink boxes (the only splash of color) to perfection. The smell of fresh-baked wholesome brownies, cookies and every imaginable yummy treat, wafts in the air and makes mouths water. Our customers sit at hand-finished antique barn-plank tabletops and look outside through the picture windows, to the west and south, to watch the world go by. People stroll in and out all day long. On summer days there are benches to sit on outside, to savor the sunshine and one of Kelly's cappuccinos or ice creams.

We do our best to remember all of our customers' names and favorite treats and, if it's your first time in, be prepared for a kind and genuine welcome. When you visit us, which we hope will be soon, be sure to look up at the ceiling. You'll see our story written there—but you know already how it goes: "Once upon a time there was a little girl who loved baking mud pies . . ."

Why We Eat Plant-Based Foods

Can a shift to a more plant-based diet help you live a longer, healthier and happier life? Yes, we think so!

Stand on any street corner and observe the people walking around you. You can see that a lot of our population is unhealthy, and that our addiction to fast and processed foods is taking its toll. Did you know that 50 percent of the men and 40 percent of the women in North America will get cancer in their lifetime? Did you know that, in Canada, someone has a heart attack every 38 seconds? Those numbers are frightening. We think the answer is a plant-based diet.

It's no secret that plants are good for you. It could be "superfood" cruciferous broccoli preventing cancer with its amazing antioxidants, blueberries with lutein, or carrots and pumpkins saving our eyesight with their famous attributes, or watermelon, strawberries and tomatoes that are red with the antioxidant lycopene, which helps to reduce cholesterol.

Study after study proves the antiaging and other health benefits of fruits and vegetables. They offer optimal health, prevent inflammation (the catalyst for many diseases) and sometimes even reverse chronic diseases in advanced stages. Many people are taking these recommendations to heart by increasing their consumption of plant foods as part of their everyday diet. This is wonderful but we need to get the word out even more.

Many people consume low-fat milk, yogurt, cheese, chicken, turkey, tuna, baked goods made with eggs and lard, etc. with good intentions. All the foods we think we should be eating. We see how these people look and the chronic disease that develops. They grow old before their time. Fatigued, they get frequent colds and battle energy loss every day. The whites of their eyes are not white, they need more sleep because their bodies are working hard on digesting as opposed to truly regenerating and relaxing through the night in a deep sleep. Their skin is dry and drawn and becoming calcified from eating and drinking acid-producing pasturized dairy. Sure, this type of food can be homemade from scratch with "wholesome" ingredients. But what it lacks are the optimal nutrients that come straight from plants. Human beings thrive on a plant-based diet that is natural, energy giving and rich in antioxidants, enzymes, fats, amino acids, carbohydrates, fiber and chlorophyll.

We've experienced first-hand the amazing differences that a plant-based diet can make to our lives, and we'd love to share our journeys with you.

KELLY'S JOURNEY

In 1998 I was 35 years old and Erinn was eight. I decided that I was through with beef. For me, it was just one decision in a long line of decisions toward finding the healthiest way to live. I never ate pork or veal anyway, and had learned too much about the potential ill effects of beef production and consumption to keep eating it. Beef was known to be full of unhealthy saturated fats, steroids, hormones and antibiotics. I had read that red meat was connected to the rise in colon cancer in North America. I felt sluggish and "thick" every time I ate it. As a family we gave it up and we didn't miss it! I focused our diet on a rainbow of vegetable and fruits, and proteins like cheese, eggs, chicken and fish.

In 2005 I met Ken, who is now my husband. He was in the restaurant/bar business, eating and drinking all the wrong things, and I was sidetracked into some of those bad habits, too. During the week I kept things as healthy as possible, but our weekends were spent with bottles of red wine, lots of fresh artisanal breads and too much yummy local cheese. It was romantic and wonderful but I was certainly paying for it. My health and general well-being began to be compromised. I could see it in my skin, it started to harm my digestion, and my sleep patterns were disturbed. Erinn could see it in me, too.

Soon my discipline kicked back in! And I convinced Ken to come along with me and Erinn on our journey to discover optimal health: breakfast of spinach and blueberry smoothies made with nut milks and vegan protein powder, or freshly ground almond butter on whole-grain toast; no more hydrogenated spreads, no butter, or fake peanut butter for

Ken. Almond milk, coconut milk and rice milk were staples in all of our lives. No more white sugar, white flour, or processed and pasteurized juices. Erinn was quickly learning the joys of making green smoothies and we all got to enjoy them.

The impact that the changes had on our lives was incredible, and we were keen to share our experience with others. We decided to start incorporating some healthier eating choices on the menu at Ken's restaurant. I began to develop more plant-based options: tofu scrambles, brown rice bowls, vegetarian curries made with coconut milk. At the same time we brainstormed constantly about environmentally friendly initiatives we could introduce.

We created an herb garden on the roof of the restaurant, with barrels collecting the rain to water the gardens. Happily, the moves paid off: sales at the restaurant increased by 25 percent and the veggie options soon accounted for 30 percent of total sales. Our signature dessert was Organic Spelt Carrot Cake with Tofu Cream Cheeze Frosting. It was the bestselling dessert in the restaurant. We were alive with energy and ideas; we made national TV with our story. So far, so great!

Unfortunately, my health still needed improvement. In July 2008 I was diagnosed with two masses in my liver. My family couldn't understand it. I was the health nut, always so virtuous about my food. Why had this happened to me? Toxins in the environment? In my food? Environmental or emotional stress? Whatever the cause, I needed to find it and discover how to heal. We started to search all over North America for the best possible treatments and nutrition plan, and try to determine what had caused my health to falter. I wasn't going to stop until I got the answers I needed, and I couldn't let go of my hope to get my body back to functioning the way it was meant to be. My determination to get the masses, cysts and fluid out of my liver was my only priority. I started reading everything I could get my hands on.

There was a lot of conflicting and confusing information out there but the clouds cleared for me when I read *The China Study* by T. Colin Campbell. He spent 40 years researching and conducting clinical trials to uncover the myths, lies and lobbies behind the widespread belief that there is a connection between animal-based protein and nutrition. In his book, Campbell reveals the half-truths that the cattle, corn and milk industries and other agribusiness lobbies want us to believe. At times when I was reading, I was brought to tears of anger and frustration thinking about how we have been fooled into thinking that meat is necessary to *survive*, that milk "does a body good" and that we should all "get cracking."

Thanks to T. Colin Campbell, I had an epiphany. Bear with me as this may sound obvious, but I suggest you stop and think about it. Reality check: I am exactly what I eat! There are poisonous herbicides, pesticides, growth hormones, antibiotics, pharmaceuticals and bacterial contamination and diseases found in all factory-farmed meat, poultry, fish and dairy products. I decided I didn't want any of that in my body anymore, nor in the bodies of everyone I love. The doctors had even found high levels of mercury in my body due to my high consumption of tuna. As a family we decided it was time to take the next step and give up all animal products completely.

And now? I have a clean bill of health. My kitchen is so much fun to work in (and I never fear cross-contamination with meat products). I've never felt or looked better. I feel alive and vibrant and full of energy. I sleep well and my digestion works perfectly. There are so many benefits to a plant-based diet, for you and for all the living beings that share our beautiful space on this planet.

ERINN'S JOURNEY

Growing up as my mom's only child was an incredible experience, full of delicious food, crazy inspiration and adventure galore. I was lucky enough to be exposed from a young age to an awareness of health, fitness and nutritious food—in both my mom's household and my dad's (my parents divorced before I was two years old). Both of my parents have always believed in, and practiced, eating right and living an active life, and it has had a huge influence on the way I live my life now.

I had my mom all to myself until I was about 18, when she married my stepdad, Ken. Our free time was spent baking, cooking and being adventurous with new recipes. We loved to fool my friends with our delicious snack food that was secretly healthy! I was Mom's willing and eager guinea pig, sampling all of her culinary creations. I'd have my friends over and we'd raid the kitchen. They were always checking out our fridge, with its crazy-wonderful rainbow of food, and commenting on the lack of a plastic, processed jungle inside. They couldn't find commercially produced fruit snacks, packaged cookies, mass-produced peanut butter or white-flour crackers in our kitchen. They couldn't even find milk. Our cupboards and fridge were full of homemade whole-grain cookies, raw cracker snacks, dehydrated veggies, almond milk and, yup, you guessed it: apples, grapes, oranges, raspberries, blueberries, broccoli, kale, sweet potatoes, and every other fruit and vegetable you can think of.

I grew up eating a very healthy diet, more so than most people I knew, but, it was after my mom finished reading *The China Study* and we visited Farm Sanctuary that a 100-percent plant-based diet became the natural next step for me. It was at the sanctuary that I had my aha! moment: How could I love certain animals as pets, and eat others? The shift for me was entirely an ethical one. The facts I learned about farm animals being reared for food were staggering (and we talk more about that below). I decided I wanted to be part of a solution—not a participant in the collective unconscious—and adopted a plant-based diet right away.

Around the same time I also stopped eating wheat and eating more clean food, and found I felt so much better: less bloated, more clear-headed, lighter and energetic. Now I don't crave wheat because we have so many better options at home and at the bakery, like flours that provide the same luscious texture and tenderness but don't cause the discomfort that so often results from eating wheat. I don't label myself gluten intolerant and I'm not celiac, but I know that I feel a lot healthier without wheat in my diet.

And now? Life is busy and beautiful, running the Kelly's Bake Shoppe empire. Our success hasn't come without some sacrifice through: Being an entrepreneur in your early 20's, and working 80 hours a week, leaves little room for normalcy—staying out until the wee hours of the morning with friends was virtually non-existent for me! I've grown up quickly and learned the fast-paced life of owning my own business. Now, six years after Kindfood began, I'm really working on finding the right balance, and taking time out to grow as a person. I'm a diehard yogi and practice six or seven days a week. Every day I meditate on gratitude, joy, love and fun. Because if we're not having fun, what's the point of all of this? Our purpose in life is to enjoy and make the most out of our time here. I make a point every day to center myself and say out loud, "Today, I will have fun." Immediately I feel a massive rush of love come over me, and it takes a huge weight off of my shoulders. Then I jump in with both feet to lead the Kelly's Bake Shoppe tribe!

MAKE ENVIRONMENTALLY INFORMED CHOICES

We all have choices: choices about our health, diet and lifestyle, and choices about the impact we make on our planet. We can choose to eat animal products and be responsible for their suffering, or not. We can choose to live on a clean and thriving planet, or continue to destroy it. We can choose to be a part of the solution or part of the problem.

Eating mostly plants is a great decision for the well-being of the environment on our planet. The meat and dairy industries are responsible for one-third of all CO_2 emissions in our atmosphere. That is something we cannot ignore. Worldwide, about 70 billion farm animals are reared for food each year. It takes 2,500 gallons of water to raise one pound of beef, and livestock consume one-third of the global grain harvest. What if we used those resources to help feed the world instead of overfeeding only some of us? Wouldn't that be better?

Not eating meat reduces the use of precious water resources, cuts down on manure accumulation and helps to stop pharmaceutical runoff in our streams, lakes and oceans. It simply doesn't make sense to *funnel* food through animals. The resources (grain and corn) that feed factory-farmed animals could be used to feed the more than one billion starving people on this planet (one in nine people are without food). The regeneration of natural farmland and forests that comes with organic and plant-based farming is critical to our survival and to the future of all living things.

Now that we truly understand the ethical and environmental damages caused by consuming animal ingredients, we feel it is our ethical imperative to commit to not eating them.

WHAT SHOULD I EAT?

At home, we eat a plant-based, mostly gluten-free diet, that is about 50% raw. By plant-based we mean we eat no animal products, including dairy and eggs. Sometimes we eat 80 percent raw, other days it's closer to 30 percent. We adjust the balance, depending on how we're feeling and the season. For us, cold weather calls for cooked comfort food, and in the summer we're more inclined to drink raw, pressed juices and eat more salads and fresh fruits. It changes all the time but what never wavers is our true addiction to a rainbow diet of vegetables.

In the next section, we give you more detailed advice about what should be in your pantry, fridge and freezer, but here is a quick summary of the foods to focus on for optimal health:

- Fresh, organic green vegetables—aim for at least 4 to 5 cups per day
- Fresh, organic red and orange vegetables—aim for at least 2 cups per day
- Fresh and dried organic fruit—an apple a day will do fine
- Non-dairy, unsweetened, organic milks: almond, rice, hemp, oat, flax, coconut
- Organic grains: quinoa, brown rice, spelt, buckwheat, millet, amaranth
- Organic legumes and beans: chickpeas, lentils, black beans, kidney beans
- Organic raw nuts
- Organic raw cacao
- Organic healthy oils: coconut oil, palm oil, avocado oil, nut oils, extra virgin olive oil, non-GMO expeller-pressed canola oil
- Organic tempeh and miso—fermented soy is easily digestible and the best way to eat soy

If you're dining out, there are several cuisines that are great for plant-based diets: Thai, Vietnamese, Indian, Japanese and Ethiopian are some of our favorites. These cuisines can accommodate vegetarians and vegans easily, and are so delicious!

How We Eat: Sample Weekday and Weekend Menus

A Typical Weekday

First thing in the morning	12 ounces of spring or filtered water with a squeeze of lemon juice
Breakfast	**Energy-Boosting Green Smoothie** with scoop of protein powder (make a double batch) and/or **Simply Delicious Granola** with hemp or unsweetened almond milk and unsweetened almond milk yogurt
Morning Snack	filtered water (don't forget your 8 glasses a day!), **Energy-Boosting Green Smoothie** left over from breakfast and a handful of **Simply Delicious Granola**
Lunch	**Savory Cheese Biscuits** and **Best-Ever Caesar Salad** with avocado slices on top
Afternoon Snack	raw apple slices or **Chocolate Chia Pudding** with blueberries
Dinner	**Original Buddha Rice Bowl** topped with **Brazil Nut "Parmesan"** and **Massaged Kale Salad**
Evening Snack	**Granola Bar**

A Typical Weekend

First thing in the morning	12 ounces of spring or filtered water with a squeeze of lemon juice
Breakfast	**Carrot Cake Smoothie**, **Easy Sunday Morning French Toast** with maple syrup and **Cashew Cream**, and fruit salad
Morning Snack	filtered water, **World Peace Cookie** and apple slices
Lunch	**Mega Salad** and **Easy Avocado Toast**
Dinner	**Moroccan Lentil Soup** with gluten-free toast and a side salad
Evening Snack	air-popped popcorn seasoned with spices

The weekend is a great time to make food for the week and a light Sunday dinner, too. Plenty of the recipes in this book are perfect to prepare ahead of time to use later in the week. These are our favorites:

- Moroccan Lentil Soup
- Lemon-Basil Lasagna
- Brazil Nut "Parmesan"
- Simply Delicious Granola
- Granola Bars

WHAT ABOUT PROTEIN?

This is one of the most common questions people ask. As a meat eater, you might have bacon and eggs for breakfast, a chicken salad sandwich for lunch and salmon with sweet potatoes and corn for dinner. Sounds pretty good, based on common dietary beliefs, but in reality you will have consumed too much animal-based protein and animal-based fat and cholesterol. Only 6 to 9 percent of our diet should be protein. For decades we have all been led to believe that we need a diet that is 20 to 30 percent protein.

Humans require 20 amino acids to make protein. Think of amino acids as the building blocks of a protein molecule (which is essential to live and build health). Of these 20 amino acids, there are eight we cannot produce ourselves (called essential amino acids) and two more are difficult for the body to produce in large enough numbers. We must supplement this deficiency of essential amino acids by eating highly nutrient-dense food.

It's easy enough to look in a biology textbook and discover that all the amino acids humans need can be found in plant foods. Look at hemp seeds, for example. These are bona fide superfoods, alive and bursting with health, and they contain every amino acid we need to maintain our health, including the eight essential amino acids and essential fatty acids (EFAs). Outside of these superstar exceptions, variety is key. We shouldn't be looking for one plant food to supply us with all of the essential amino acids we need, but a diet made up of a variety of plant foods will most definitely meet our protein needs and enable us to thrive.

Bottom line: eat enough and a good variety of whole plant foods, and your amino acid/protein needs will be easily met.

Plant-based Cooking & Baking

Home cooking requires organization, the right tools and—crucially important—staple ingredients close at hand. You don't need to totally reinvent your grocery list to enjoy a plant-based diet but you'll find it much easier to eat delicious, varied meals and snacks if you have a few key basics in your cupboards, fridge and freezer.

Try to buy local, seasonal, non-genetically-modified ingredients whenever possible. We always buy organic to avoid pesticides, food additives, chemical ripening and food irradiation, and we encourage you to do the same. Even cane sugar should be organic as the white conventional type is processed with animal bones and bleach.

At home, at Kelly's Bake Shoppe, and at Lettuce Love Cafe, we use only gluten-free ingredients. We wanted our Bake Shoppe to offer something for everybody with a food allergy or intolerance. When we discovered that we could cook and bake with alternatives to wheat that are healthier, better tasting and packed with nutrients, we didn't think twice! Flours such as fava bean and chickpea are high in fiber, protein and iron. They also retain moisture very well . . . goodbye, dry muffins! So they're better for us and they're superstar ingredients in the bakery. What's not to love?

THE PLANT-BASED PANTRY

All of these ingredients are readily available in grocery stores. Nothing listed below requires ordering online. Easy! Here is a sampling of must-haves for our home kitchens, please choose organic wherever possible:

In the cupboard

Baking ingredients
arrowroot starch
baking powder (aluminum-free)
baking soda
coconut sugar
gluten-free oats (we love Bob's Red Mill or Cream Hill certified wheat-free)
gluten-free vegan chocolate chips (we love Enjoy Life)
organic cane sugar (never conventional)
Sucanat (evaporated cane juice)
tapioca starch
xanthan gum

Beans & legumes
black beans (canned and dried)
cannellini beans (canned and dried)
chickpeas (canned and dried)
kidney beans, white and red (canned and dried)
lentils, green and red (dried)
navy beans (canned and dried)
refried beans (canned)

Canned goods
coconut milk
tomatoes (we prefer San Marzano)

Dried spices & herbs
allspice
basil
black pepper
cayenne pepper
chipotle chili powder
cinnamon
cloves
coriander seeds
cumin seeds
curry powder
ginger
ground coriander
ground cumin
Himalayan sea salt
nutmeg
oregano
red chili flakes
rosemary
thyme
turmeric

Flours
almond flour
brown rice flour
coconut flour
garbanzo bean flour
garbanzo and fava flour
gluten-free all-purpose flour
oat flour
quinoa flour
sorghum flour
sweet rice flour
teff flour

Miscellaneous
apple cider vinegar
balsamic vinegar
gluten-free crackers (we love Mary's)
granola
low-sodium vegetable stock
lucuma powder and syrup
maca powder (raw)
meal-replacement powder (we love Vega and Sunwarrior)
protein powder (we love Sunwarrior or Vega)

Oils
avocado oil
canola oil (expeller-pressed non-GMO)
coconut oil
hemp oil
non-hydrogenated palm shortening
non-hydrogenated vegan shortening
olive oil
sunflower seed oil

Pasta
brown rice lasagna noodles
buckwheat pasta
gluten-free pasta (quinoa and brown rice)
sweet potato pasta

Rice & grains
arborio rice
brown rice
millet
quinoa

In the refrigerator

Butters
raw almond butter
vegan butter (we love Earth Balance)

Dried fruit, seeds & nuts
almonds (raw and unpasteurized)
blueberries
cashew nuts (raw)
cherries
chia seeds
cranberries
goji berries
hemp seeds (raw)
pumpkin seeds (raw)
raisins
sunflower seeds (raw)
walnuts (raw)

Milks
almond milk
coconut milk
hemp milk
oat milk
rice milk
soy milk

Miscellaneous
Dijon mustard
non-dairy yogurt
nutritional yeast
olives
organic peanut butter (never conventional)
stone-ground mustard
tamari (wheat free)
tempeh (we like Noble Bean)
tofu
vegan cream cheese
vegan mayonnaise (we love Vegenaise)

Syrups & sweeteners
agave syrup
coconut sugar
coconut syrup
honey (raw, preferably from a sustainable local apiary. See page 82)
jam (sweetened with grape juice)
maple syrup
organic cane sugar (never conventional)
Sucanat (evaporated cane juice)

In the freezer

corn tortillas
ground flax seed
flax seeds
gluten-free quinoa or buckwheat bread
organic fruits and vegetables (an assortment!)
. . . and the occasional brownie or cookie from Kelly's Bake Shoppe!

BECOMING A PLANT-BASED BAKER

Plant-based baking simply means baking with no animal products, such as lard, butter, eggs, dairy and even some white sugars. For decades we were conditioned to think that we must bake with eggs, butter, cream and other dairy. What are chocolate chip cookies without the richness of butter and eggs? What about a quiche or pancakes without eggs, or a chocolate cake baked without milk and eggs? Well, we're here to prove to you that baking without animal ingredients is healthier for you and even tastes better and fresher. The easy substitutions are simple and more nutritious. For some, this prospect may sound daunting but when done right—and it is so easy—it becomes second nature. Most people who try it really enjoy the new taste and texture . . . and they love rediscovering their taste buds.

This approach to baking is also wonderful for the waistline: there are no trans fats, no indigestible animal-fat cholesterol, no worry of contamination from animal-based products, no anxiety about expiry dates, no added hormones or antibiotics nor pharmaceutical steroids. Plant-based baking uses natural, whole plant-based foods with an abundance of nutrition. Most substitutes are high in fiber, too.

So, how can you bake without the ingredients you're used to? With easy plant-based ingredient substitutions! Eggs? We've got you covered. Butter? No problem. Milk and cream? Let's try ditching them, shall we? To start off, it's important to understand what each of these animal-based ingredients does for the baked good. What property are we trying to replace?

Plant-Based Ingredient Substitutes

Eggs

These bring moisture to a baked good. Eggs also bind and leaven in baking. For example, eggs work well for leavening cakes but for cookies they act more as a binder. You'll find that cookies, cakes and muffins are so easy to make without animal-based ingredients, you'll wonder why you ever used eggs before.

In a nutshell, you need to assess the recipe and know what the eggs were meant to do so that you can pick the right substitute. Whether the egg substitute is for cookies or cakes or a vegan quiche or maybe even a veggie burger, you can't just use one replacement for all.

Flax: This is a great binder. We use ground flax seed as a substitute for eggs, and it's always successful. Mix the filtered water and ground flax seed together and let it sit for at least 5 minutes before using. That way it thickens and turns into more of a gelatinous egg-like consistency. This is great for cookies, veggie burgers, nut loaves or brownies.

1 tablespoon ground flax seed + 3 tablespoons filtered water = 1 egg

🍃 **Chia seeds:** These are an incredible binder and they act the same way ground flax seed does. The very cool thing about chia seeds is they also provide crunch to cookies or to a cake or even to pancakes.

1 tablespoon chia seeds + 3 tablespoons filtered water = 1 egg

🍃 **Applesauce or mashed banana:** Used as a substitute for eggs, these both encourage moist results. We also increase the baking powder or baking soda (or both) in the recipe, so that whatever we're baking will rise. Applesauce and mashed banana increase the sweetness and for some recipes, like banana bread, that's a great thing.

¼ cup applesauce or ½ banana (mashed) + ½ teaspoon baking powder = 1 egg

🍃 **Sweet potato purée:** This is the perfect egg substitute to enhance chocolate cake bases. Removing the eggs and adding ¼ cup of sweet potato purée will add richness and moisture to baking. Again, you will need to increase the quantity of baking soda or baking powder if you require the baked good to rise.

¼ cup sweet potato purée + ½ teaspoon baking powder = 1 egg

🍃 **Arrowroot starch/tapioca starch/cornstarch/potato starch:** Starches can be used in cookies as a substitute for eggs. Starch will bind without resulting in the dark spots ground flax seed causes. There is no need to change anything else in the recipe; simply add the starch to the dry mix. Here's the egg replacer we use in the bakery and call for in some of the recipes in this book:

1 tablespoon arrowroot starch + 3 tablespoons filtered water = 1 egg

🍃 **Coconut milk yogurt:** We love this egg substitute for pancakes and cakes. It makes everything fluffy, moist and supple, the way perfect pancakes should be.

¼ cup unsweetened coconut milk yogurt = 1 egg

🍃 **Silken tofu:** Use this in puddings and brownies and other dense baked goods that do not need to rise much. Because silken tofu is heavier and thicker, it will work best in more substantial baked goods. It's a great substitute when you're making French toast or brownies, but don't use it in something like vanilla cupcakes or they could turn out like hockey pucks.

¼ cup silken tofu (must be blended with the wet ingredients in the recipe) = 1 egg

🍃 **Firm and extra-firm tofu:** This (non-GMO, of course) is a staple at Lettuce Love Café and in our fridges at home. This is the only way to make delicious scrambled "eggs" (scrambled tofu) and vegan quiche. The texture of this type of tofu is essential to making the perfect egg for breakfast. Add some sautéed onion, spices and turmeric for a lovely yellow color.

1 cup of tofu = 1 cup eggs (about 3 eggs)

Butter

Butter is one of the easier animal-based ingredients to replace. It's as simple as adding vegan butter, such as our fave Earth Balance, to the recipe in equal parts to the butter you're replacing.

1 cup vegan butter = 1 cup butter

Lard

Lard is made from pigs. We have never used it in any of our cooking or baking, proving how unnecessary it is. When we have seen a request for it in a recipe, we ignore it and add vegan non–hydrogenated shortening usually made from a mixture of tropical oils, like palm or coconut. We use sustainable palm shortening that comes from small farms and does not hurt the orangutan's natural habitat. We use only Spectrum Organics because it has been certified sustainable by RSPO (Roundtable on Sustainable Palm Oil), which believes in sustaining resources for all our futures. Spectrum purchases their oil from the Daabon Organic Group, which is globally recognized as a leader in sustainable farming in Colombia.

Milk and cream

Who'd have thought it would be so easy to make the milk switch? We've been so conditioned to think that milk brings flavor and richness to cooking and baking that it almost paralyzes us with fear to make the change. It's hard to overcome the childhood conditioning that "milk does a body good." It's been 20 years (maybe more) since I have had a glass of milk. I can honestly say I don't miss it. I enjoy my almond milk or hemp milk or coconut milk in so many more flavorful ways. We always buy unsweetened varieties. We love almond and coconut milk on their own and in smoothies and lattes.

✐ **Baking:** We use unsweetened rice milk (flavorless) and unsweetened almond milk (rich flavor) and unsweetened coconut milk (rich flavor) in baking.

✐ **Mayonnaise:** We use non-GMO soy milk in our vegan mayonnaise, and nothing else will do. We have tried numerous plant-based milks and it is impossible to thicken mayonnaise using any other milk substitute.

✐ **Sauces:** Cheese-type sauces are best created and thickened with soy milk. We've tried others, and the sauce doesn't turn out as thick and creamy as when made with soy milk. Be sure to find non-GMO soy milk made from organic beans. We also use our own homemade Cashew Cream (page 85) and find that having it on hand is a required staple in the plant-based pantry. Of course unsweetened hemp milk, unsweetened coconut milk and unsweetened almond milk can be used, too. They all have unique and stronger flavors than soy milk. Depending on the recipe, feel free to use whatever flavor you'd like. For example, for curry dishes, we use canned coconut milk in the sauces and for some soups we will use unsweetened coconut milk or cream, or cashew cream.

Are You Living Your Life Yet?

Are you living your life yet? That's what we ask ourselves every day. It's a reality check, a reminder to stay present and to focus on what's important and *live your life*, because no one else is doing it for you.

For us, life is about inspiring and sharing our love and passion for healthy, whole plant-based foods with as many people as possible. In the café and Bake Shoppe we serve delicious, healthy alternatives, both savory and sweet. Everything we make is gluten-free, meat-free, dairy-free, egg-free, peanut-free and made using plant-based organic, natural ingredients. The natural flavors we use include organic cocoa, applesauce, lemons, peppermint oil, espresso beans, agave and coconut, which include natural colors sourced from flower petals and other plants. Why use artificial ingredients when Mother Nature makes the most yummy flavors and colors?!

We are truly committed to a better way of eating, and inspiring a better way to live. That's why we're so excited to be able to share our recipes with you. You will see that we have highlighted our absolute favorite recipes throughout the book, shown by either a 🧡 (Kelly's favorite) or 💙 (Erinn's favorite). These are the recipes we love the most, for the go-to foods we love to cook when cravings hit. Our recipes truly are our prized possessions, so please enjoy them, love them as much as we do and share them with all your friends and family.

Savory Moments

Vanilla Almond Milk (page 26)

Drinks & Smoothies

KELLY'S BIKINI SEASON TONIC   24

CHOCOLATE HEMP MILK   24

VANILLA ALMOND MILK   26

RED VELVET SHAKE   27

CARROT CAKE SMOOTHIE   29

PUMPKIN PIE SMOOTHIE   29

ERINN'S ENERGY-BOOSTING GREEN SMOOTHIE   31

PIÑA COLADA SMOOTHIE   31

CACAO BLUEBERRY SMOOTHIE   32

CHOCOLATE CRUNCH SMOOTHIE   35

KELLY'S BIKINI SEASON TONIC

♥ This was a best-seller at Kindfood from the day we opened. Women, especially, love that it helps them to lose body fat. It's perfect for the summer or any time you think you need a quick detox. Chosen for their fat-flushing properties, these ingredients will make you feel vibrant and healthy.

Active time: 5 minutes

Total time: 6 minutes

Makes 2 servings

1 red grapefruit, peeled and quartered

2 red apples, cored and quartered

2 cups kale, including stems

½ cup fresh mint leaves

1 lemon, peeled and halved

1. In the order they are listed, add the grapefruit, apples, kale, mint and lemon to a juicer.
2. Juice, then serve as soon as possible to get the maximum vitamin C from the citrus fruits.

By juicing in this order, the lemon cleans out the machine and pushes through the mint and kale.

CHOCOLATE HEMP MILK

We are addicted to this delicious, nutritious non-dairy milk. It can be served cold or warm but be careful not to let it come to a boil or the enzymes and nutrients will be destroyed. For vanilla hemp milk, omit the cacao powder.

Active time: 8 minutes

Total time: 10 minutes

Makes 2 servings

6 tablespoons hemp seeds

2 tablespoons maple syrup

1 tablespoon raw cacao powder

1 teaspoon vanilla extract

Pinch of sea salt

1. In a heavy-duty blender on high speed, combine 2 cups of filtered water with the hemp seeds, maple syrup, cacao powder, vanilla and salt. Blend for 2 minutes or until smooth.
2. If you'd like to serve the hemp milk warm, pour it into a small saucepan and warm gently for about 3 minutes. Watch closely to ensure it doesn't boil.

VANILLA ALMOND MILK (photo on page 22)

This is such a simple, useful recipe and making your own almond milk means you can control the ingredients. If you love vanilla, use more! We like Himalayan sea salt but you can choose whatever high-quality sea salt you prefer. The cinnamon is comforting and will help your digestion.

Active time: 10 minutes

Total time: 8 hours of soaking time, plus 15 minutes

Makes 4 cups

1 cup raw almonds

3 soft Medjool dates, pitted

2 teaspoons vanilla extract

¼ teaspoon ground cinnamon

Pinch of fine sea salt

1. In a medium bowl, cover the almonds with 2 cups of filtered water. Refrigerate the almonds and filtered water to soak overnight.

2. Drain the almonds, then rinse well and drain again. Tip the almonds into a heavy-duty blender and add 3 ½ cups of filtered water. Blend on high speed for about 2 minutes.

3. Hold a nut-milk bag open over a large bowl and slowly pour the almond milk mixture into the bag. Gently squeeze the bottom of the bag to release the milk through the cloth. This will take 2 to 3 minutes.

4. Rinse out the blender. Return the now filtered almond milk to the blender, with the dates, vanilla, cinnamon and salt. Blend on high speed to combine.

5. Pour the almond milk into a glass jar with a lid. Store in the refrigerator for up to 5 days. Shake the jar well before using; the mixture separates over time.

A nut-milk bag is a small fine-mesh bag usually made of nylon. They are reusable, inexpensive and easy to find; you can almost certainly get one from your local health food store.

If the dates are very dry or hard, soak them in lukewarm filtered water for about 20 minutes to soften before using.

RED VELVET SHAKE (photo on page 28)

Talk about a twist of fun here. Can this really be healthy? Nutritious? Who would've thought that?! Most people would never think of blending ice cream and beet juice, but we're here to change the way you think about shakes!

Active time: 5 minutes
Total time: 5 minutes
Makes 3 servings

3 cups vanilla bean non-dairy ice cream

1 frozen banana, peeled and cut into
    1-inch pieces

½ cup beet juice

½ cup non-dairy milk

3 tablespoons raw cacao powder

2 tablespoons vanilla or chocolate
    protein powder

2 tablespoons cacao nibs

1. In a heavy-duty blender on high speed, blend the ice cream, banana, beet juice, milk, cacao powder, protein powder and cacao nibs until very smooth.

2. Share with two others, maybe three . . .

DID YOU KNOW?

Beet juice is the fitness world's newest natural energy drink. Some studies are showing that it gives athletes an extra edge in endurance and speed, taking precious seconds off performance times. Beetroot is naturally high in nitrates which the body converts into nitric oxide, a gas that actually widens blood vessels. The widening blood vessels bring more oxygen to muscles, thus increasing athletic efficiency. We could all benefit from a beet boost to oxygenate our brains and bodies!

Top to bottom:
Pumpkin Pie Smoothie,
Carrot Cake Smoothie,
Red Velvet Shake (page 27)

DID YOU KNOW?

It's been more than a decade since we stopped drinking pasteurized juices. Pasteurization involves heating to kill any harmful bacteria, but the process also kills healthy nutrients. In our opinion, even the organic varieties of juice are not worth buying because pasteurization takes away the "living" properties of the juices. There's power in whole food, enjoyed as close to its original state as possible.

CARROT CAKE SMOOTHIE

This was known as the Bunny Smoothie back in our Kindfood days. We always make our own fresh carrot and ginger juice as it's so easy to do. With the cinnamon and banana, this smoothie tastes like that classic dessert we can't resist!

Active time: 5 minutes
Total time: 5 minutes
Makes 2 servings

2 large carrots, peeled

1-inch piece fresh ginger, peeled

1 cup Vanilla Almond Milk (page 26) or
    store-bought unsweetened almond milk

1 frozen banana, cut into 1-inch pieces

½ avocado, pitted

1 tablespoon unsweetened shredded coconut

Pinch of ground cinnamon

1. In a juicer, juice the carrots and the ginger just before you make the smoothie.
2. In a heavy-duty blender on high speed, blend ⅔ cup carrot-ginger juice with the vanilla almond milk, banana, avocado, coconut and cinnamon until smooth.
3. Serve immediately.

PUMPKIN PIE SMOOTHIE

Flavorful and rich in beta-carotene and fiber, pumpkin is super nutritious. We like this made with a frozen banana for a thick, luxurious texture, but it's okay to use an unfrozen one. This is a festive smoothie that's perfect for Thanksgiving or Christmas morning.

Active time: 3 minutes
Total time: 5 minutes
Makes 2 servings

1 ½ cups Vanilla Almond Milk (page 26) or
    store-bought unsweetened almond milk

1 ½ frozen bananas, peeled and cut into
    1-inch pieces

1 cup pumpkin purée

3 tablespoons maple syrup

1 tablespoon chia seeds

½ teaspoon ground cinnamon

½ teaspoon ground nutmeg

½ teaspoon ground allspice

1. In a heavy-duty blender on high speed, blend the vanilla almond milk, bananas, pumpkin purée, maple syrup, chia seeds, cinnamon, nutmeg and allspice for 1 minute, or until smooth and frothy.
2. Pour into glasses and enjoy!

VARIATION

To pump up the protein and really make this a meal, add 2 tablespoons vegan vanilla protein powder.

ERINN'S ENERGY-BOOSTING GREEN SMOOTHIE

This is one of our favorite go-to smoothies. It's loaded with vitamins and minerals. Substituting coconut water for regular water gives this—and you—a huge electrolyte blast. Great for beating that afternoon slump or recovering after a workout.

Active time: 5 minutes
Total time: 5 minutes
Makes 2 servings

2 cups coconut water

2 frozen bananas, peeled and cut into
    1-inch pieces

½ cup spinach

½ cup kale, tough stems removed

2 Medjool dates, pitted

1-inch piece fresh ginger, peeled

2 teaspoons whole flax seeds

2 teaspoons chia seeds

2 teaspoons hemp seeds

1 teaspoon ground cinnamon

1. In a heavy-duty blender on high speed, blend the coconut water, bananas, spinach, kale, dates, ginger, flax, chia, hemp and cinnamon for about 1 minute, or until smooth and creamy.

2. Pour into glasses and enjoy.

PIÑA COLADA SMOOTHIE

We really like piña colada smoothies but we don't like getting caught in the rain! Bad song jokes aside, this is a taste of sunshine that will really pick up your morning, especially in the darker winter months when we need an extra boost of vitamin C (from the citrus) and digestive enzymes (from the pineapple).

Active time: 3 minutes
Total time: 5 minutes
Makes 1 serving

1 frozen banana, cut into 1-inch pieces

½ orange, peeled, segmented and frozen

1 peeled pineapple spear, cut into large
    chunks and frozen

½ cup unsweetened rice or almond milk

⅔ cup canned coconut milk

1 tablespoon unsweetened shredded coconut

1. In a heavy-duty blender on high speed, blend the banana, orange, pineapple, rice and coconut milks and shredded coconut for 1 minute, or until frothy and smooth. (You may want to blend a second time if you don't like your smoothie chunky.)

2. Serve ice cold.

The frozen fruit in this smoothie makes it icy cold and thick.

CACAO BLUEBERRY SMOOTHIE

There is so much goodness in this smoothie. Each of the ingredients has super-nutritional benefits and super-yummy flavor. Bet you didn't know that blueberries activate the fat-burning gene in abdominal fat cells. Really! Blueberries are also excellent for eyesight because of the high levels of lutein found in them. This is a smoothie designed for anti-aging Goddesses, so indulge in these beautiful purple creations.

Active time: 5 minutes
Total time: 5 minutes
Makes 2 servings

2 cups unsweetened coconut milk

¾ cup frozen blueberries

1 frozen banana, peeled and cut into
    1-inch pieces

½ avocado, pitted

¼ cup raw cashews (optional)

2 tablespoons cacao nibs

2 tablespoons rice bran solubles
    (see sidebar)

1 tablespoon chia seeds

1 tablespoon raw cacao powder

1 teaspoon MSM (see sidebar)

1. In a heavy-duty blender on high speed, blend the coconut milk, blueberries, banana, avocado, cashews (if using), cacao nibs, rice bran solubles, chia seeds, cacao powder and MSM for about 2 minutes, or until smooth.

2. Pour into glasses and enjoy the raw plant and mineral power coursing into your system.

DID YOU KNOW?

MSM (methylsulfonylmethane) is an organosulfur compound. Sulfur is one of the five chemical elements that are vital to optimal health and are found in every cell in our bodies. Sulfur helps to process antibodies, hormones and enzymes, to synthesize collagen and to produce immunoglobin.

Rice bran solubles (aka tocotrienols) are amazing and delicious. They should be a part of everyone's daily diet due to their outstanding ability to protect our cells. Nerve-related cell damage can happen over time, resulting in poor stress tolerance, memory loss and impaired cognitive skills. Pollution, excess stress, toxic food and cosmetics, food colorings, MSG and pesticides can induce chronic nerve cell damage.

CHOCOLATE CRUNCH SMOOTHIE

This smoothie is full of antioxidants and the healthy fats that are so necessary for our brain and cellular development. It also tastes like the deep, dark chocolate milkshake of your dreams! Check out some of the optional add-ins below.

Active time: 5 minutes
Total time: 5 minutes
Makes 1 serving

1 cup Vanilla Almond Milk (page 26) or
    store-bought unsweetened almond milk
1 ½ frozen bananas, peeled and cut into
    1-inch pieces
3 Medjool dates, pitted and softened
2 tablespoons raw cacao powder
1 tablespoon cacao butter
1 tablespoon coconut oil
3 tablespoons cacao nibs

1. In a heavy-duty blender on high speed, blend the vanilla almond milk, bananas, dates, cacao powder, cacao butter and coconut oil until smooth.
2. Add 2 tablespoons of the cacao nibs to the blender and pulse. Don't blend too much; you want the cacao nibs to retain their crunch.
3. Pour into a glass and sprinkle with remaining cacao nibs. Serve as soon as possible. You won't be able to wait, anyway!

VARIATIONS:

- Add 2 scoops chocolate protein powder.
- Add 1-inch piece fresh ginger, peeled (chocolate with ginger is divine).
- Add half a pitted avocado.
- Add 1 tablespoon organic raw almond butter (or sunflower butter for those with nut allergies).

DID YOU KNOW?

Did you know that chocolate and cacao are not the same? Raw cacao has 400 times the antioxidants of processed cocoa or chocolate. Cacao contains the lipid anandamide, which causes changes in blood pressure and blood-sugar levels, leading to feelings of excitement and alertness. Yes, cacao makes us feel joy and is believed to be an aphrodisiac.

The secret to Lettuce Love Café's rich and creamy smoothies is the addition of frozen ripe bananas to the mix.

Waffles (page 47)

Breakfast & Brunch

SIMPLY DELICIOUS GRANOLA

This granola is perfect mixed with coconut yogurt, blended with a smoothie, or eaten as a snack right from your lunch bag while at school or on the road. We use this healthy granola as the crunchy topping on our Pumpkin Breakfast Muffins (page 177). It is a shelf staple and can be kept in the cupboard in an airtight container for two to four weeks, but it only lasts a couple days 'round here!

Active time: 15 to 20 minutes

Total time: 60 minutes

Makes 8 servings

1 ½ cups gluten-free oats

½ cup roughly chopped raw almonds

½ cup roughly chopped raw Brazil nuts

½ cup roughly chopped raw walnuts

½ cup raw pumpkin seeds

½ cup raw sunflower seeds

1 tablespoon chia seeds

1 teaspoon ground cinnamon

½ teaspoon sea salt

¼ cup coconut oil, melted

½ cup maple syrup

2 tablespoons brown rice syrup

1 tablespoon vanilla extract

¼ cup dried cranberries

¼ cup dried goji berries

¼ cup Thompson raisins

2 tablespoons hemp seeds

1. Preheat the oven to 300°F. Line a large, heavy baking sheet with parchment paper.

2. In a medium bowl, combine the oats, almonds, Brazil nuts, walnuts, pumpkin seeds, sunflower seeds, chia seeds, cinnamon and salt.

3. In a small saucepan over low heat, warm the coconut oil. Add the maple and brown rice syrups, vanilla and 2 tablespoons of filtered water. Stir to combine.

4. Pour the wet ingredients over the dry ingredients and stir with a wooden spoon.

5. Pour the granola onto the prepared baking sheet, making sure it's evenly distributed.

6. Bake the granola for about 30 minutes, stirring after 15 minutes. Add the dried fruit and hemp seeds. Bake for another 10 minutes, or until the granola is golden brown and clusters begin to form.

7. Allow the granola to cool and get nice and crunchy before serving or storing.

> **DID YOU KNOW?**
> Many people who are trying to avoid gluten don't realize that packaged rolled oats often contain gluten that's introduced in the processing stages. Oats don't naturally contain gluten and there are more brands of gluten-free rolled oats available now. We use Bob's Red at the Bake Shoppe.

EASY AVOCADO TOAST

🖤 + 💚 This is one of our favorite recipes to keep us going on those 14-hour days. Avocados are loaded with healthy fats that help our brains stay sharp and our bodies lean. Substitute avocado for traditional peanut butter on toast and add a little sea salt for your new food addiction.

Active time: 5 minutes
Total time: 5 minutes
Makes 2 servings

2 slices gluten-free bread

2 teaspoons vegan butter or coconut oil

1 avocado, pitted and sliced

Pinch of sea salt

Pinch of red chili flakes (optional)

Balsamic reduction (optional)

1. Toast the bread slices on both sides, then spread one side of each with vegan butter.

2. Arrange the sliced avocado on the buttered toast.

3. Sprinkle evenly with salt. Sprinkle with red chili flakes (if using) and drizzle with balsamic reduction (if using). Enjoy!

EASY SUNDAY MORNING FRENCH TOAST

💚 French toast is a Lettuce Love Café classic but it's a challenging dish for cooks who are trying to make plant-based, gluten-free meals. Breakfast in general is difficult if you're avoiding animal products. Erinn developed this recipe at home to satisfy Mike's insatiable cravings for French toast, which he missed after he adopted a plant-based diet.

Active time: 15 minutes

Total time: 15 minutes

Makes 4 servings

1 ¼ cups non-dairy milk

¾ cup organic raw almond butter

⅓ cup maple syrup, plus more to serve

¼ cup plus 1 tablespoon gluten-free
    all-purpose flour

1 tablespoon ground cinnamon

1 tablespoon vanilla extract

¼ teaspoon ground nutmeg

Pinch of sea salt

4 tablespoons vegan butter

8 slices gluten-free bread

¼ cup pecans, chopped

Maple syrup (for serving)

1. In a large shallow dish, combine the non-dairy milk, almond butter, ⅓ cup maple syrup, flour, cinnamon, vanilla, nutmeg and salt.

2. Heat a large skillet over medium heat. Add 1 tablespoon of vegan butter and heat until it sizzles.

3. Dip the bread into the almond butter mixture, one slice a time, and let it soak briefly, for 10 to 15 seconds.

4. Fry the bread slices, in batches, for 4 to 5 minutes per side or until golden brown, adding more vegan butter to the skillet as necessary.

5. Serve sprinkled with pecans and drizzled with maple syrup (or try topping with our Whipped Cashew Cream (page 195) or Whipped Coconut Cream (page 196)).

You can prepare the batter ahead of time and refrigerate it for 2 to 3 days.

Clockwise from top left:
Savory; Lemon, Blueberry & Cinnamon;
Chocolate Monkey (page 46); Mango & Coconut

BASIC PANCAKES

Pancakes aren't just for breakfast anymore. Although we love them with just a drizzle of maple syrup, we also experiment with chocolate and banana, or mashed sweet potato and miso gravy, or . . . you get the idea.

Active time: 15 minutes

Total time: 15 minutes

Makes 12 pancakes

1 ¼ cups brown rice flour

1 cup gluten-free all-purpose flour

1 tablespoon Sucanat

½ teaspoon baking soda

½ teaspoon sea salt

2 tablespoons ground flax seed

1 tablespoon chia seeds

1 ½ cups plain unsweetened coconut milk yogurt

1 ¼ cups Vanilla Almond Milk (page 26) or
    store-bought unsweetened almond milk

1 tablespoon olive oil

1 teaspoon lemon zest

1 teaspoon fresh lemon juice

1 teaspoon vanilla extract

Nonstick cooking spray

1. In a large bowl, whisk together the rice and all-purpose flours, Sucanat, baking soda and salt.

2. In a small bowl, mix the ground flax seed with 6 tablespoons of filtered water and set aside to thicken.

3. In another small bowl, mix the chia seeds with 3 tablespoons of filtered water and set aside.

4. In a medium mixing bowl, mix the flax and chia mixtures with the yogurt, almond milk, oil, lemon zest and juice, and vanilla.

5. Add the wet ingredients to the dry ingredients and stir just until blended. The batter will be slightly thick, not runny.

6. Heat a large skillet over medium-low heat. Remove the skillet from the heat and film with cooking spray. Add ¼-cup portions of the batter to the skillet. Cooking 3 pancakes at once is easiest.

7. Flip the pancakes when they are lightly browned on the underside and can be lifted easily. They will puff up as they cook. When lightly browned on the second side, remove the pancakes from the skillet and serve immediately.

VARIATIONS:

Savory Pancakes

1. In step 1, add a pinch of ground black pepper, ¼ teaspoon dried basil and ½ teaspoon dried thyme.

2. In step 4, only use unsweetened almond milk and omit the vanilla essence.

3. Top with Chipotle Mashed Sweet Potatoes (page 96), Miso Gravy (page 97) and sprigs of rosemary.

Lemon, Blueberry & Cinnamon Pancakes

1. Increase the lemon zest and juice to 1 tablespoon each.

2. In step 1, add ½ teaspoon ground cinnamon to the dry ingredients.

3. In step 4, fold in ½ cup fresh or frozen blueberries.

Mango & Coconut Pancakes

1. In step 4, add ¼ cup peeled, pitted and chopped mango and 2 tablespoons shredded coconut.

2. Top with Whipped Cashew Cream (page 195).

CHOCOLATE MONKEY PANCAKES (photo on page 44)

These pancakes are a classic from Erinn's childhood and she insisted we share them with you. Every kid of any age deserves homemade Chocolate Monkey Pancakes on Sunday morning for wonderful magical memories.

Active time: 20 minutes
Total time: 30 minutes
Makes 6 large pancakes

1 tablespoon coconut oil, plus more
    if necessary
1 recipe Basic Pancakes (page 45) batter
2 bananas, peeled and sliced ¼-inch thick
½ cup vegan chocolate chips

1. Add a little coconut oil to a large skillet and heat over medium-high heat.
2. Ladle ⅔ cup of the batter into the skillet and gently smooth the pancake with the back of the ladle.
3. Cover the pancake with one-sixth of the bananas and chocolate chips. Cover the skillet and let the pancake cook through. Do not flip it. Cook for about 5 minutes or until the top is not gooey. The pancake will be brown on the bottom when you peek under it.
4. Remove the pancake from the skillet and serve immediately or keep warm in a 250°F oven while you make the rest of the pancakes, adding more coconut oil to the skillet as necessary.

WAFFLES

This variation on our pancake recipe makes tender-crisp waffles that you can enjoy with sweet or savory toppings. Really! Try waffles piled high with garlic-sautéed greens, a mound of mashed potatoes and a ladleful of vegan gravy: you'll be in comfort-food heaven. Or top them with a big dollop of our Whipped Cashew Cream (our whipped cream substitute, page 195), some fresh berries and a drizzle of maple syrup.

Active time: 10 minutes

Total time: 30 minutes

Makes 12 waffles

1 ¼ cups brown rice flour

1 cup gluten-free all-purpose flour

1 tablespoon Sucanat

½ teaspoon baking soda

½ teaspoon sea salt

2 tablespoons ground flax seed

1 tablespoon chia seeds

1 ½ cups plain unsweetened coconut milk yogurt

1 ¼ cups Vanilla Almond Milk (page 26) or store-bought unsweetened almond milk

2 tablespoons olive oil

1 teaspoon vanilla extract

Coconut oil spray for greasing

1. In a large bowl, whisk together the rice and all-purpose flours, Sucanat, baking soda and salt.

2. In a small bowl, mix the ground flax seed with 6 tablespoons of filtered water and set aside to thicken.

3. In another small bowl, mix the chia seeds with 3 tablespoons of filtered water and set aside to thicken.

4. In a large glass measuring cup or pitcher, mix the flax and chia mixtures with the yogurt, almond milk, oil and vanilla.

5. Add the wet ingredients to the dry ingredients and stir just until blended. The batter will be slightly thick, not runny.

6. Heat a waffle iron on medium heat. Grease the iron. Add about ½ cup of batter (depending on the size of your waffle iron) and slowly close the lid.

7. Cook for 3 to 4 minutes or until steam stops rising from the waffle iron. Remove and serve immediately. Repeat with the remaining batter.

For savory waffles, omit the Sucanat from step 1.

CHOCOLATE CHIA PUDDING

Do you remember having tapioca as a kid? Well, it was one of our favorites! When we stumbled upon chia pudding, it was life changing. Chia seeds are packed with omega-3 fatty acids, and provide fiber and calcium that tapioca doesn't. And you don't need to cook chia pudding! It's perfect for breakfast, dessert or a light snack, and has become a staple in our kitchen.

Active time: 5 minutes

Total time: 1 to 2 hours of refrigeration, to chill and thicken

Makes 4 servings

2 cups chilled unsweetened coconut milk or
    other non-dairy milk

½ cup chia seeds

5 tablespoons raw cacao powder

5 tablespoons maple syrup or 6 tablespoons
    yacón syrup

1 teaspoon vanilla bean powder or
    1 tablespoon vanilla extract

Pinch of sea salt

1. In a small bowl, whisk the coconut milk, chia seeds, cacao powder, syrup, vanilla and sea salt.
2. Cover and refrigerate for 2 hours.

VARIATIONS:

- For Mexican Spice Chia Pudding, add a pinch each of cayenne pepper and ground cinnamon.
- Add 1 scoop vanilla or chocolate protein powder for a perfect protein hit.
- Add 3 tablespoons of organic peanut butter, but don't mix it in completely, leave some ribbons.
- Add 1 tablespoon Giddy Yoyo Raw Red Banana Powder to amp up vitamins C and B_6, and potassium and fiber.

DID YOU KNOW?

Omega 3 fatty acids are very important for brain health. Chia seeds have five grams of omega 3 fatty acids per one ounce serving.

Fettuccine Alfredo (page 69)

Lunch & Dinner

CAULIFLOWER WINGS WITH SRIRACHA SAUCE   53

LOVE 'N' PEAS MUFFINS   54

YUMMY VEGAN QUICHE   57

GRILLED CHEESE SANDWICH   59

TEMPEH REUBEN   60

SWEET POTATO & QUINOA BURGERS   63

NUT, QUINOA & MILLET LOAF   64

TEMPEH CHILI   65

ORIGINAL BUDDHA RICE BOWL   67

BAKED MAC 'N' CHEESE   68

FETTUCCINE ALFREDO   69

LEMON-BASIL LASAGNA   70

CAULIFLOWER WINGS WITH SRIRACHA SAUCE

We've created a savory, gluten-free batter to dip vegetables in before baking them until crisp. But it's really the Sriracha that makes this dish addictive: it's all in the sauce! The wings are also delicious served with our vegan Ranch Dressing (page 100) and carrot and celery sticks on the side.

Active time: 30 minutes
Total time: 45 minutes
Makes 6 servings

¾ cup plus 1 tablespoon unsweetened
    almond milk or filtered water
⅔ cup gluten-free all-purpose flour
½ cup oat flour
1 tablespoon agave syrup
2 teaspoons garlic powder
½ teaspoon dried basil
Pinch of sweet smoked paprika (see page 63)
Pinch of cayenne pepper
Pinch of sea salt
1 head cauliflower, chopped into
    1-inch florets
Sriracha Sauce (page 98)
Ranch Dressing (page 100)

1. Preheat the oven to 450°F. Line a large baking sheet with parchment paper.
2. In a medium bowl, whisk the almond milk, all-purpose and oat flours, agave syrup, garlic powder, basil, smoked paprika, cayenne and salt until the mixture is the consistency of thin pancake batter. Add more almond milk or filtered water to get it just right; you don't want it too thick.
3. Toss the cauliflower in the batter to coat the florets. Using your hands, place the battered cauliflower on the prepared baking sheet. Bake in the center of the oven for 15 to 20 minutes, flipping the florets halfway through baking to ensure even browning.
4. In a medium saucepan, heat the Sriracha sauce over medium heat for about 5 minutes or until bubbling. Remove from the heat and set aside.
5. Tip the cooked cauliflower into a large bowl. Toss the cauliflower with enough of the sauce to evenly coat it, reserving the remaining sauce to serve as a dip.
6. Return the coated cauliflower to the baking sheet and bake for 5 to 7 more minutes, or until the florets are crispy. Serve the cauliflower immediately with the remaining Sriracha sauce and some ranch dressing for dipping.

> **DID YOU KNOW?**
> Huy Fong Sriracha sauce was the invention of David Tran, a Vietnamese refugee in the U.S. In 1980, he was homesick for a hot sauce good enough to eat on pho, the traditional Vietnamese soup. Now Sriracha sauce is ubiquitous, with imitators springing up daily and inventive new products being developed, like Sriracha-flavored potato chips and even beer.

LOVE 'N' PEAS MUFFINS

We developed this muffin at Kindfood as a lunch special for kids. The inspiration for the name came from a T-shirt slogan Kelly saw and loved in California. Moms would buy these muffins for their kids' lunches and snacks at Lettuce Love Café, knowing they would get something fun, nutritious and yummy. We now sell them at Kelly's Bake Shoppe, and they're not just for kids. This is a perfect lunch muffin to take along when you're brown-bagging it.

Active time: 10 minutes

Total time: 45 minutes

Makes 12 muffins

Coconut oil or nonstick cooking spray

⅔ cup unsweetened rice milk

4 tablespoons ground flax seed

2 cups gluten-free all-purpose flour

¾ cup coconut sugar or Sucanat

½ cup oat flour

2 teaspoons baking powder

2 teaspoons baking soda

1 teaspoon ground cinnamon

1 teaspoon sea salt

½ teaspoon xanthan gum

½ cup sunflower seed oil, canola oil or
     olive oil

¼ cup maple syrup

2 tablespoons molasses

2 teaspoons vanilla extract

1 ½ cups butternut squash purée

1 cup defrosted frozen peas or fresh peas

¼ cup chopped walnuts (optional)

2 heaping scoops vanilla protein powder
     (optional)

FOR THE OAT STREUSEL TOPPING:

¼ cup coconut sugar

3 tablespoons gluten-free rolled oats

2 tablespoons oat flour

2 tablespoons vegan butter

1. Preheat the oven to 350°F. Spray a 12-cup muffin pan with coconut oil or cooking spray or line with paper liners.

2. In a small bowl, combine the rice milk and ground flax seed and set aside, to thicken.

3. In a medium bowl, whisk together the all-purpose flour, coconut sugar, oat flour, baking powder, baking soda, cinnamon, salt and xanthan gum.

4. In another medium bowl, mix the sunflower seed oil, maple syrup, molasses and vanilla. Stir in the rice milk mixture.

5. Add the dry ingredients to the wet ingredients. Blend with an electric hand mixer until fully combined.

6. Fold in the butternut squash purée and stir gently to combine. Gently fold in the peas. Add the walnuts and protein powder (if using).

7. Using an ice-cream scoop, spoon the batter into the prepared muffin pan.

8. To make the streusel topping (if using), mix the coconut sugar, rolled oats, oat flour and vegan butter with a fork or your fingertips until the mixture is crumbly. Sprinkle on top of muffins.

9. Bake for 22 to 25 minutes, or until a cake tester inserted into the center of a muffin comes out clean. Allow to cool for 10 minutes before removing the muffins from the pan.

YUMMY VEGAN QUICHE

This recipe proves that you can do anything you set your mind to. When our publisher challenged us to create a quiche recipe without animal products, we took up the challenge with gusto. We promise you won't miss the eggs! For convenience we would never frown on anyone for using a store-bought pie crust. Try to find a vegan version, please!

Active time: 30 minutes
Total time: 60 minutes
Makes one 9-inch quiche

1 unbaked 9-inch Gluten-Free Pie Crust
    (page 106)

1 package (14 ounces) firm tofu

½ cup Cashew Cream (page 101)

4 tablespoons nutritional yeast

2 tablespoons soy or coconut milk creamer

2 tablespoons chickpea flour

1 tablespoon arrowroot starch

1 teaspoon dried parsley

1 teaspoon dried basil

1 teaspoon red chili flakes (or more if you
    like spicy heat)

¾ teaspoon ground turmeric

½ teaspoon sea salt

¼ teaspoon ground black pepper

2 tablespoons olive oil or coconut oil

1 medium yellow onion, diced

1 cup sliced cremini or white mushrooms

2 tablespoons finely chopped sun-dried
    tomatoes

2 cloves garlic, minced

1 ½ cups fresh spinach

½ cup shredded non-dairy cheddar-
    or mozzarella-style cheese

2 teaspoons vegan "bacon" bits (optional)

1. Prepare the gluten-free pie crust.

2. Preheat the oven to 375°F.

3. In a food processor, combine the tofu, cashew cream, nutritional yeast, creamer, chickpea flour, arrowroot starch, parsley, basil, chili flakes, turmeric, salt and pepper. Process until smooth. If it seems too thick, add a tablespoon or two of filtered water. Pour the mixture into a large bowl.

4. In a medium skillet, heat the olive oil over medium-high heat. Sauté the onion for about 5 minutes, or until translucent and starting to brown. Add the mushrooms, sun-dried tomatoes and garlic and sauté for a few more minutes, or until the mushrooms are soft.

5. Add the onion mixture to the tofu mixture and stir well. Add the spinach, non-dairy cheese and "bacon" bits (if using). Stir until blended.

6. Pour the quiche mixture into the pie crust and smooth it out with a spatula.

7. Bake for 30 to 35 minutes, or until a knife inserted in the center of the quiche comes out clean. The crust edges should be golden brown. Let sit for 10 minutes, then cut and serve.

GRILLED CHEESE SANDWICH

This is an all-time favorite with our customers at the café. We actually call it "The OMG." It's comfort food to the max that will satisfy the little kid in you and we love it paired with our Tomato Protein Soup (page 76). We tried to take it off the menu once and there was a massive customer revolt. Every step in this method is important, so don't skip a beat.

Active time: 10 minutes
Total time: 15 minutes
Makes 2 servings

4 slices gluten-free bread

4 tablespoons vegan butter

4 tablespoons Chipotle Eggless Mayo
    (page 100)

½ cup shredded non-dairy cheddar-style
    cheese

4 tablespoons shredded non-dairy
    mozzarella-style cheese

1. Heat a large skillet over medium heat. Butter one side of each slice of bread. Place the 4 slices of bread in the skillet, butter side *up*. Cook for 1 minute and then flip the slices.

2. Spread the mayo on two slices of bread. Top these slices with the non-dairy cheddar and mozzarella.

3. Place the other bread slices, buttered sides *up*, on the top of the cheese. This way the cheese gets warm and melted quickly.

4. Cover the skillet and cook for 2 minutes. Lift the lid and check to see if the bread has browned on the underside. When it's nicely browned, flip it over and cook, covered, for another 3 minutes.

5. Serve with your preferred condiments and a nice crunchy pickle, if you have one.

TEMPEH REUBEN

This sandwich was created to satisfy Kelly's husband's love of the classic deli favorite. Ken missed his favorite deli sandwich when he went to an entirely plant-based diet. It was Kelly's mission to try to recreate this sandwich without any meat or dairy. Mission accomplished!

Active time: 25 minutes
Total time: 40 minutes
Makes 4 servings

FOR THE MARINADE:

¼ cup dill pickle or sauerkraut juice

½ lemon, juiced

2 tablespoons beet juice

2 tablespoons olive oil

⅛ teaspoon minced garlic

FOR THE RUSSIAN DRESSING:

½ cup Eggless Mayo (page 100) or Vegenaise

¼ cup organic ketchup

2 tablespoons finely diced, drained
    dill pickles

1 teaspoon finely diced red onion

¼ teaspoon garlic powder

⅛ teaspoon organic stone-ground mustard

FOR THE TEMPEH:

1 package (8 ounces) tempeh

2 tablespoons olive oil

½ cup shredded non-dairy cheddar-style
    cheese

8 slices gluten-free bread

1 cup sauerkraut, drained

1. To make the marinade, whisk the pickle juice, lemon juice, beet juice, olive oil and garlic in a small bowl. (You could also process the mixture in a small food processor for 5 seconds, or until combined.) Pour the marinade into a baking dish large enough to hold the tempeh slices in one layer. Set aside.

2. To make the dressing, combine the mayo, ketchup, dill pickles, red onion, garlic powder and mustard in a small bowl. Set aside.

3. Heat a steamer pot. Once hot, steam the tempeh for about 5 minutes, or until it swells and plumps up slightly. (Steaming opens up the tempeh and allows it to absorb more flavor from the marinade.)

4. Take the tempeh out of the steamer, place it on a cutting board and let it cool. Cut the cooled tempeh in half so you have 2 rectangular blocks. Slice each rectangular block through the middle to make 4 thin rectangles.

5. Place the tempeh in the marinade and marinate the pieces on each side for at least 15 minutes or up to overnight. (The marinated tempeh can be removed from the marinade and stored in the fridge for up to 2 days.)

6. Heat a heavy skillet over medium heat and add the olive oil. Sear the tempeh slices for about 4 minutes per side, or until slightly browned.

7. Sprinkle non-dairy cheddar on each slice of tempeh, then cover the skillet and cook for 3 to 4 minutes to melt the cheese. Meanwhile, toast the bread and keep the toast warm.

8. Put 4 slices of toast on a flat surface, then top each slice with 2 tablespoons of the dressing, 3 tablespoons of the sauerkraut and 1 slice of tempeh. Top the tempeh with another tablespoon of sauerkraut and a drizzle of dressing. The more gooey the better! Top with the remaining slices of toast and serve, making sure there are plenty of napkins within reach.

Try to use unpasteurized sauerkraut for a healthier option.

SWEET POTATO & QUINOA BURGERS

We call these "clean" burgers because they are light and fresh and you won't feel guilty when you go for a second one. We fell in love with burgers like these when we were at a yoga retreat in Ibiza, Spain. When we got back home we couldn't wait to recreate them! You can get a head start by prepping the quinoa and sweet potatoes the day before you want to serve them.

Active time: 25 minutes

Total time: 70 minutes

Makes 8 burgers

2 sweet potatoes, peeled and cubed, or
   ¾ cup sweet potato purée

1 cup quinoa, rinsed and drained

½ cup oat flour

½ cup chopped fresh cilantro

2 green onions, finely chopped

1 tablespoon ground flax seed

1 clove garlic, minced

1 teaspoon grated fresh ginger

1 teaspoon ground cumin

1 teaspoon sweet smoked paprika
   (see sidebar)

½ teaspoon dried basil

Sea salt and ground black pepper to taste

1 tablespoon olive oil

8 gluten-free burger buns

OPTIONAL TOPPINGS:

Avocado slices

Lettuce leaves

Tomato slices

Red onion slices

Chipotle Eggless Mayo (page 100)

Cilantro aioli

Guacamole

1. If you are using cubed raw sweet potatoes, preheat the oven to 375°F. Line a baking sheet with parchment paper. Spread the sweet potatoes out in a single layer and roast for about 25 minutes or until soft. In a large bowl, purée the sweet potatoes by hand or with a hand mixer.

2. Cook the quinoa according to the package directions. Mix the quinoa into the freshly made or ready made sweet potato purée and stir well.

3. Add the oat flour, cilantro, green onions, ground flax seed, garlic, ginger, cumin, paprika, basil, and salt and pepper. Combine the mixture well with your hands then form into four burgers.

4. In a large, heavy skillet, heat the olive oil over medium-high heat. Fry the burgers for about 6 minutes on each side, or until they're golden brown.

5. Serve on gluten-free buns with optional toppings (but not ketchup or mustard or relish).

Smoked paprika has a deeper, more assertive flavor than regular paprika. It's an awesome spice that comes in different heat levels, ranging from sweet through hot. Larger supermarkets should have it, but you may need to buy it at a specialty food store.

NUT, QUINOA & MILLET LOAF

This delicious veggie loaf is a family tradition every Christmas, and something we look forward to at holiday time. We use any leftovers in sandwiches, with sliced avocado and tomato and a dab of Chipotle Eggless Mayo (page 100), or crumble the leftover loaf over a salad. Scrumptious!

Active time: 45 minutes
Total time: 3 hours
Makes 6 to 9 servings

Olive oil for greasing
1 small butternut squash, peeled, seeded
    and cut into 1-inch chunks
3 tablespoons olive oil
1 cup dried green lentils, rinsed and drained
1 tablespoon sea salt
½ cup millet
½ cup quinoa, rinsed and drained
1 large onion, diced
3 cloves garlic, minced
2 stalks celery, diced
2 medium carrots, diced
1 tablespoon chopped fresh rosemary leaves
1 tablespoon chopped fresh thyme leaves
1 teaspoon dried basil
½ teaspoon red chili flakes
1 cup gluten-free oats
¼ cup finely ground raw almonds
4 tablespoons nutritional yeast
2 tablespoons yellow miso paste, thinned
    with 2 tablespoons filtered water
2 teaspoons dried parsley
Sea salt and ground black pepper to taste

1. Preheat the oven to 375°F. Grease a 9- x 5-inch loaf pan. Line a roasting pan with parchment paper.

2. In a bowl, toss the squash with 2 tablespoons of the olive oil. Transfer the squash to the prepared roasting pan and roast, uncovered, for 30 minutes, or until very well browned. (The browner the better, as this will give the loaf a very earthy flavor.) Set the squash aside until cool, then purée it in a food processor or blender until smooth.

3. In a medium saucepan, bring 4 cups of water to a boil. Add the lentils and salt, and boil for 5 minutes. Reduce the heat to medium-low, cover and simmer for 10 minutes.

4. Add the millet to the saucepan and simmer, covered, for 20 more minutes (be sure to set the timer). Stir in the quinoa, then cover and simmer for 10 more minutes. Remove the saucepan from the heat and set aside to cool.

5. In a nonstick skillet over medium-high heat, sauté the onion in the remaining 1 tablespoon of olive oil for 2 minutes. Add the garlic and cook for 1 more minute, or until very fragrant. Reduce the heat and add the celery and carrots. Sauté for 10 minutes. Add the rosemary, thyme, basil and chili flakes. Remove the skillet from the heat and set aside.

6. Put the lentil mixture into a large bowl. Fold in the vegetable mixture. Add the oats, ground almonds, nutritional yeast, diluted miso paste and parsley. Stir in the butternut squash purée.

7. Add salt and pepper to taste. We try to avoid cooking with too much salt and pepper and prefer to add them at the table. That way, they don't mask the taste of the herbs and spices.

8. Put the loaf mixture in the prepared pan. Bake uncovered for 50 minutes. (It's important that the loaf be uncovered to allow the edges to brown.) Remove the loaf from the oven and let it cool in the pan for 5 minutes before unmolding and slicing.

TEMPEH CHILI

Our famous chili will warm you to the bone and give you a perfect hit of spice. Many a meat eater has proclaimed their love for our chili, not knowing it's meatless. We've proven a good bowl of chili doesn't need meat and now we're happy to share our secret recipe, the one that all of you have wanted to get your hands on for years.

Active time: 30 minutes
Total time: 90 minutes
Makes 10 to 12 servings

6 tablespoons olive oil

1 ½ packages (each 8 ounces) tempeh, crumbled

2 tablespoons wheat-free tamari

2 medium yellow onions, diced

3 cloves garlic, minced

1 sweet red pepper, seeded and chopped

1 sweet green pepper, seeded and chopped

3 cans (each 28 ounces) diced tomatoes

2 cans (each 15 ounces) kidney beans, drained and rinsed

½ cup frozen corn kernels (optional)

2 teaspoons chili powder

2 teaspoons ground cumin

2 teaspoons ground coriander

1 teaspoon chipotle chili powder

½ teaspoon ground allspice

½ teaspoon sea salt

½ teaspoon ground black pepper

¼ teaspoon ground cloves

1. In a large pot, heat 4 tablespoons of the olive oil over medium-high heat. Sauté the crumbled tempeh for about 5 minutes, or until golden brown.

2. Add the tamari and sauté for 5 more minutes, or until the tempeh has darkened and tastes wonderful. Remove the tempeh and set aside.

3. In the same pot, heat the remaining olive oil over medium-high heat and sauté the onions and garlic for 5 minutes, or until the onions become translucent. Add the red and green peppers and cook, stirring with a wooden spoon, for about 5 minutes, or until softened.

4. Reduce the heat to medium. Add the tomatoes (with their juice), kidney beans, corn kernels (if using), chili powder, cumin, coriander, chipotle powder, allspice, salt, pepper and cloves. Stir in the cooked tempeh.

5. Bring to a boil and reduce the heat to low. Simmer, uncovered, for at least 60 minutes and up to 90 minutes, until the chili has thickened and the flavors have deepened and developed.

6. Serve in bowls with a side of Cumin-Scented Cornbread (page 90).

ORIGINAL BUDDHA RICE BOWL

This is one of our most popular dishes at the café because it's got something of everything, and is all so delicious. We like to grill some of the veggies and leave others raw to provide a variety of flavors and textures. Grilling also brings out the natural sugars in sweet potato and red pepper, which makes this a treat in a bowl!

Active time: 15 minutes
Total time: 20 minutes
Makes 2 servings

1 sweet potato, thickly sliced

1 sweet red pepper, seeded and thickly sliced

2 tablespoons olive oil, plus extra for oiling
    the vegetables

3 cups cooked short-grain brown rice

2 tablespoons wheat-free tamari

1 teaspoon dried basil

2 tablespoons diced red onion

6 oil-packed sun-dried tomatoes, very
    finely sliced

4 slices avocado

4 tablespoons raw sunflower seeds

¼ cup chopped cilantro

12 raw almonds

1. Preheat the grill to medium-high. Brush the sweet potato and red pepper slices with olive oil. Grill for 10 to 15 minutes until tender and browned, turning the vegetables midway through cooking. Set aside.

2. Divide the cooked rice between two bowls and drizzle each portion with 1 tablespoon olive oil and 1 tablespoon tamari. Sprinkle each bowl with ½ teaspoon dried basil.

3. Arrange the grilled vegetables, red onion and sun-dried tomatoes on the rice.

4. Top with avocado slices, sunflower seeds, cilantro and 6 almonds per bowl.

BAKED MAC 'N' CHEESE

A perennial favorite in our house and at our café, this is especially good if you have vegetarian teenagers. It's amazing how a little nutritional yeast can mimic the flavor of cheese—and it's a whole lot easier on your digestion. For easier prep, measure and assemble all the ingredients before starting. And don't forget to put a bottle of ketchup on the table, too.

Active time: 20 minutes
Total time: 50 minutes
Makes 6 servings

Nonstick cooking spray

6 cups uncooked brown rice penne or
 elbow macaroni

⅓ cup vegan butter

⅓ cup olive oil

½ cup brown rice flour

6 tablespoons wheat-free tamari

2 tablespoons brown miso paste

1 tablespoon raw tahini

2 tablespoons ketchup

2 tablespoons fresh lemon juice

2 ¾ cups unsweetened soy milk
 (no substitutes or the sauce won't
 be creamy)

1 cup nutritional yeast

½ teaspoon sea salt

Ground black pepper to taste

1 cup shredded non-dairy mozzarella-style
 cheese

1. Preheat the oven to 375°F. Lightly spray a 13- x 9-inch ovenproof dish, and a piece of aluminum foil large enough to cover it, with cooking spray.

2. Fill a large pasta pot with water and set over high heat to boil. Cook the pasta according to the package directions.

3. While the pasta is cooking, make a roux by melting the vegan butter and olive oil in a saucepan over medium heat (be careful it's not too hot). Add the flour and whisk until dissolved, then continue to stir for about 2 minutes, until the flour has lost its raw flavor.

4. Add the tamari, miso, tahini, ketchup and lemon juice to the roux. Whisk well to eliminate any lumps.

5. Slowly whisk in the soy milk, making sure to scrape the sides of the saucepan.

6. Turn the heat up to medium-high. Add the nutritional yeast, salt and pepper and whisk until thick. Once the sauce starts to boil, it should be sufficiently thick.

7. Drain the pasta and return it to the pasta pot. Stir the sauce into the hot pasta until it is thoroughly coated. Pour the mixture into the prepared dish and scatter with shredded non-dairy cheese. Cover the dish tightly with the prepared foil.

8. Bake for 30 minutes or until the edges are slightly bubbly and brown. Let the mac 'n' cheese cool for about 10 minutes before serving.

Nutritional yeast is grown on molasses. It's full of necessary B-complex vitamins, including B_{12} (that herbivores are normally low on), and is a source of protein containing all 18 amino acids. B vitamins help balance our emotions and minimize depression, insomnia, fatigue, PMS, mood changes and irritability. They also improve memory, and strengthen skin, hair and nails.

FETTUCCINE ALFREDO (photo on page 50)

Traditionally an alfredo sauce is made with a whole lot of dairy: rich, heavy cream *and* cheese. Our version is kinder to the planet and your waistline. We turn to this when we want to have a real stick-to-your-ribs meal. Please be sure to use coconut milk or soy milk; if made with almond or rice milk, the sauce isn't as deliciously thick.

Active time: 15 minutes
Total time: 20 minutes
Makes 4 servings

1 pound brown rice fettuccine noodles

1 tablespoon olive oil

1 tablespoon minced shallot

2 cloves garlic, minced

¾ cup almond milk

½ cup vegetable broth

1 ½ cups cauliflower florets

½ cup raw cashews

3 tablespoons nutritional yeast

1 ½ tablespoons lemon juice

½ teaspoon Dijon mustard

½ teaspoon wheat-free tamari

Pinch of sea salt

Pinch of paprika (optional)

Pinch of ground nutmeg

Chopped fresh parsley for garnish

1. Fill a large pasta pot with water and bring to a boil over high heat. Cook the noodles according to the package directions. Drain and return to the pasta pot.

2. Heat the oil in a large saucepan over medium heat. Sauté the shallots and garlic for 3 to 4 minutes.

3. Add the almond milk and vegetable broth. Lower the heat once the liquid begins to simmer. Add the cauliflower and cook for 6 to 7 minutes, or until the cauliflower is soft. Add the cashews and nutritional yeast and stir for a minute.

4. Remove the saucepan from the heat. Transfer the cauliflower mixture into a blender. Add the lemon juice, Dijon mustard, tamari, salt, paprika (if using) and nutmeg. Blend, on high speed, for about 30 seconds, or until smooth.

5. Gently stir the sauce into the noodles over low heat. Heat for a minute or so, until the sauce is warmed through. Divide evenly among four bowls and garnish with parsley. Serve with a side of gluten-free garlic bread and watch the smiles.

LEMON-BASIL LASAGNA

This recipe takes a bit of time, but it's worth it. It is a great make-ahead dish when you're feeding a crowd, and the portions are generous!

Active time: 90 minutes
Total time: 10 hours (including resting)
Makes 8 servings

FOR THE VEGETABLES:

1 tablespoon olive oil

1 ½ yellow onions, finely chopped

4 cloves garlic, minced

1 ½ pounds cremini mushrooms, chopped

2 zucchini, chopped

2 sweet red peppers, seeded and chopped

1 cup spinach leaves, chopped

FOR THE CHEESE SAUCE:

3 cups raw cashews

4 cups basil leaves

1 ⅓ cups nutritional yeast

⅔ cup vegetable broth

⅔ cup fresh lemon juice

4 tablespoons Dijon mustard

6 cloves garlic, peeled

4 teaspoons sea salt

FOR THE LASAGNA:

Nonstick cooking spray

1 pound gluten-free brown rice lasagna
   noodles

3 cups Tomato Basil Sauce (page 98) or good
   quality store-bought marinara sauce

1 cup shredded non-dairy mozzarella-style
   cheese

¼ cup basil leaves, sliced into ribbons

1. To prepare the vegetables, heat the oil in a large skillet over medium heat. Sauté the onions and garlic for 5 minutes, or until fragrant.

2. Add the mushrooms, zucchini and peppers. Sauté for 10 minutes, or until the vegetables release their liquid. Add the spinach and sauté for 5 more minutes.

3. Remove the skillet from the heat. Tip the veggies into a stainless steel bowl and refrigerate overnight. This is a very important step: overnight the vegetables will release a tremendous amount of liquid which you don't want in your finished lasagna.

4. To make the cheese sauce, put the cashews in a small bowl with enough filtered water to cover them, then refrigerate for about 30 minutes.

5. Drain the cashews and rinse well. In a heavy-duty blender on high speed, blend the cashews, basil, nutritional yeast, veggie broth, lemon juice, mustard, garlic and salt for 2 to 4 minutes, or until smooth. Set aside.

6. To make the lasagna, preheat the oven to 400°F. Lightly spray a 13- x 9-inch ovenproof dish, and a piece of aluminum foil large enough to cover it, with cooking spray. Fill a large pasta pot with water and set over high heat to boil. Cook the lasagna noodles according to the package directions. Drain.

7. Drain the vegetable mixture well. Spread 1 cup of the tomato basil sauce over the bottom of the prepared baking dish. Cover with a layer of noodles. Spread 1 cup of cheese sauce over the noodles, then top with half of the drained vegetables. Repeat the layers of tomato basil sauce, noodles and veggies, ending with a final layer of noodles, then tomato basil sauce. Sprinkle non-dairy mozzarella over the top.

8. Cover the baking dish with the prepared aluminum foil, cutting a few vents in the foil to allow steam to escape during cooking. Bake for 45 minutes or until the lasagna is bubbling.

9. Remove the foil and put the lasagna under the broiler for 5 to 7 minutes to brown. Watch it closely so the edges don't burn. Allow the lasagna to cool and set for about 10 minutes before serving.

10. Serve garnished with the basil and drizzled with remaining cheese sauce.

Soups & Salads

CREAMY BUTTERNUT SQUASH SOUP

Doesn't this sound warm and soothing? Well, it tastes just as good. Butternut squash roasts to a melting sweetness that's emphasized by the maple syrup and coconut milk we add at the end of cooking. This is a great choice if you're feeding kids, especially if they're veggie-averse. The flavor will *squash* any reluctance! This soup works well with our Savory Cheese Biscuits (page 91).

Active time: 25 minutes
Total time: 1 ½ hours
Makes 10 to 12 servings

Nonstick cooking spray
2 large butternut squash
4 tablespoons olive oil
½ teaspoon ground cinnamon
2 medium yellow onions, diced
½ teaspoon red chili flakes
6 cloves garlic, minced
2 tablespoons grated fresh ginger
1 teaspoon sea salt
8 cups vegetable broth
½ cup canned coconut milk
2 tablespoons maple syrup

1. Set the oven to 375°F. Spray two baking sheets or roasting pans with cooking spray.

2. Halve the squash and remove the seeds. Lightly brush each half with a little of the olive oil and sprinkle with cinnamon. Place the squash on the baking sheets, skin-side up, and cover tightly with foil. Bake for 45 to 60 minutes, or until the squash has softened. Feel free to uncover the squash and turn them over for the last 5 minutes.

3. Meanwhile, heat the remaining olive oil in a stockpot over medium heat. Sauté the onions for 3 minutes, or until translucent. Add the chili flakes and sauté for 3 more minutes. Add the garlic, ginger and salt, and sauté for 2 minutes, or until fragrant. Remove the pot from the heat.

4. When the squash is ready, remove it from the oven and let cool for 15 minutes. Scoop the squash out of the skin and add to the pot, along with the veggie broth.

5. Return the pot to medium heat and bring to a simmer. Simmer for about 15 minutes to allow the flavors to combine and deepen. Add the coconut milk and maple syrup.

6. Blend the soup, in batches, until smooth. (Don't overfill the blender or you risk scalding yourself and making a mess of your kitchen counter!) Return the soup to the pot and heat through. The soup can be refrigerated for up to 5 days and also freezes well.

When the squash is ready, it will be very easy to scoop out of its skin, so make sure you roast it until it's beautifully soft.

TOMATO PROTEIN SOUP

This is so creamy, delicious and satisfying, you won't even care that it's also packed with nutrients and fiber. Tomatoes are an important source of lycopene which, in some studies, has been shown to reduce the risk of cancers and age-related diseases. Factor in the chickpeas' high protein and fiber content and you've got a super-soup!

Active time: 20 minutes

Total time: 30 to 35 minutes

Makes 6 to 8 servings

2 tablespoons olive oil

2 medium yellow onions, diced

3 large cloves garlic, minced

1 ½ teaspoons ground turmeric

1 teaspoon ground cumin

1 teaspoon red chili flakes

2 cans (each 15 ounces) chickpeas,
     drained and rinsed

2 cans (each 28 ounces) diced tomatoes

3 cups vegetable broth

1 teaspoon sea salt

½ teaspoon ground black pepper

4 tablespoons nutritional yeast

Fresh cilantro sprigs for garnish

Gluten-free bread croutons for garnish

1. Heat the oil in a large stockpot. Add the onions and sauté for 3 minutes, or until translucent. Add the garlic and sauté for another couple of minutes, until there's a wonderful aroma but the garlic isn't browning.

2. Add the turmeric, cumin and chili flakes, and stir for 1 minute. Add the chickpeas and sauté until they begin to turn golden brown and are coated with the spices.

3. Add the tomatoes (with their juice), veggie broth, salt and pepper, and bring to a boil. Simmer for 10 to 15 minutes.

4. Blend the soup, in batches, until smooth, adding the nutritional yeast to the first batch. (Don't overfill the blender, as hot liquids expand while blending and you run the risk of scalding yourself and making a mess of your kitchen counter!) Return the soup to the pot and heat through.

5. Serve garnished with sprigs of cilantro and gluten-free croutons. Soup may be refrigerated for up to 5 days.

MOROCCAN LENTIL SOUP

This is a wonderfully fragrant and delicious soup with a depth of flavor that comes from toasting the cumin and coriander seeds. Toasting really brings out the character of the spices. We often make a double batch of this soup so there will be easy meals in the freezer.

Active time: 25 minutes
Total time: 60 minutes
Makes 10 to 12 servings

3 tablespoons plus 1 teaspoon cumin seeds

2 tablespoons coriander seeds

½ cup diced onion

3 tablespoons olive oil

2 teaspoons red chili flakes

2 teaspoons curry powder

2 teaspoons minced garlic

10 to 11 cups vegetable broth

3 ½ cups dried red lentils, rinsed and drained

2 cups diced carrots

1 cup diced celery

4 tablespoons peeled and minced
    fresh ginger

1 teaspoon ground black pepper

3 cups canned coconut milk

1 cup chopped fresh cilantro

Grated zest of 2 lemons

2 tablespoons fresh lemon juice

1 teaspoon sea salt

Fresh cilantro leaves for garnish

1. In a dry stockpot over medium heat, toast the cumin and coriander seeds for 2 to 3 minutes, or until fragrant, giving them a little stir to encourage even cooking.

2. Add the onion, olive oil, chili flakes, curry powder and garlic to the pot. Cook, stirring constantly, for about 5 minutes, or until the onion becomes soft and translucent.

3. Stir in the veggie broth, lentils, carrots, celery, ginger and pepper. Bring to a simmer, then cover and simmer for 30 to 40 minutes, or until the carrots are tender and the lentils are soft.

4. Blend the soup, in batches, until smooth. (Don't overfill the blender or you risk scalding yourself and making a mess of your kitchen counter!)

5. Return the soup to the pot. Stir in the coconut milk, cilantro, lemon zest and juice, and salt. Stir and heat for 5 minutes. (Try not to let the soup boil, as this could make the coconut milk split. If this happens the soup will look a bit curdled, but don't worry, it will still taste good.) Serve garnished with cilantro.

CELERY ROOT & GREEN APPLE SOUP

Some people shy away from celery root, aka celeriac, because of its gnarled, bulbous appearance. But this root vegetable tastes fresh and savory—like a combination of celery and parsley—which makes it a yummy addition to soups or salads. Containing potassium, calcium and fiber, it's a healthy addition, too.

Active time: 30 to 35 minutes
Total time: 40 to 45 minutes
Makes 6 to 8 servings

1 tablespoon olive oil

1 medium onion, chopped

1 leek, white and pale green parts only, diced

2 cloves garlic, minced

2 stalks celery, chopped

1 green apple, cored and chopped

2 to 3 cups vegetable broth

2 large celery roots, peeled and cut into
    1-inch pieces

1 cup diced cauliflower

1 cup unsweetened coconut milk

1 teaspoon sea salt

1 teaspoon fresh lemon juice

Ground black pepper to taste

Diced green apple for garnish

Canned coconut milk or Cashew Cream
    (page 101) for garnish

1. In a 10-quart stockpot, heat the olive oil over medium-high heat. Sauté the onion, leek and garlic for about 6 minutes, or until the onion begins to brown slightly. Add the celery, chopped apple and ½ cup filtered water, and sauté a few more minutes to soften the vegetables.

2. Add 2 cups of the veggie broth, the celery roots and cauliflower. Increase the heat to high, cover the pot and bring to a boil. Reduce the heat to medium and simmer, covered, for 10 to 12 minutes, or until the vegetables are tender. (The vegetables should be just covered with the broth; if not, add more broth.)

3. Transfer about one-third of the vegetables and liquid to a blender. Add ⅓ cup of the coconut milk and purée until smooth. Repeat with the remaining soup and coconut milk. Return the blended soup to the stockpot and bring to a simmer.

4. Stir in the salt, lemon juice and pepper, adjusting the seasonings if needed. Warm the soup gently and serve garnished with diced green apple and a swirl of coconut milk or cashew cream.

LENTIL & GREENS DETOX SOUP

 We really must insist you use the freshest organic vegetables possible for this soup. You can only detox by using nontoxic ingredients, so please don't ingest pesticides or genetically modified crops for this soup. Your body will thank you for it!

Active time: 20 minutes

Total time: 40 to 45 minutes

Makes 8 to 10 servings

1 tablespoon olive oil

1 red onion, diced

2 large cloves garlic, minced

3 stalks celery, diced

½ cup diced carrot

2 teaspoons chili powder

1 teaspoon ground cumin

1 teaspoon ground turmeric

½ teaspoon sweet smoked paprika
    (see page 63)

¼ teaspoon cayenne pepper (optional)

1 bay leaf

6 cups vegetable broth

1 can (28 ounces) chickpeas, drained
    and rinsed

1 can (28 ounces) diced tomatoes

1 cup dried red lentils, rinsed and drained

½ cup red quinoa, rinsed and drained

3 teaspoons sea salt

½ teaspoon ground black pepper

2 handfuls kale leaves, roughly torn

2 handfuls Swiss chard leaves, roughly torn

1. In a 10-quart stockpot, heat the oil over medium heat. Sauté the onion and garlic for 5 to 6 minutes, or until the onion softens and turns translucent. Add the celery and carrot, and sauté for a few more minutes until the vegetables start to turn brown at the edges.

2. Stir in the chili powder, cumin, turmeric, paprika, cayenne (if using) and bay leaf.

3. Stir in the veggie broth, chickpeas, tomatoes (with their juice), lentils and quinoa.

4. Bring to a boil, then reduce the heat and simmer, uncovered, for 20 to 25 minutes, or until the lentils are tender and fluffy.

5. Stir in the kale and chard leaves, then remove the pot from the heat. Season to taste and enjoy!

Make a double batch of this soup; leftovers can be stored in the freezer for up to a month.

Turmeric is a widely used spice in Asia, where its familiar rich yellow color makes curries and stews look beautiful and taste delicious. Turmeric contains curcumin, long used as a powerful liver detoxifier. Curcumin is also known for its powerful antioxidant, anti-inflammatory properties.

MASSAGED KALE SALAD

By now, you know kale is the queen of dark, green leafy vegetables, with amazing health benefits. If kale works so hard for us as a nutritional powerhouse, why not show it a little love? Massaging the leaves (for two to three minutes) tenderizes them and makes them more digestible. We always have kale on hand and eat it about a million times a week.

Active time: 15 minutes
Total time: 15 minutes
Makes 2 to 3 servings

1 large bunch green kale, torn into
      bite-size pieces

4 tablespoons olive oil

¼ teaspoon sea salt, plus a bit for the dressing

1 large carrot, grated

½ cup raisins or dried goji berries

4 teaspoons sesame seeds

4 teaspoons hemp seeds

2 teaspoons minced red onion

Grated zest and juice of 1 lemon

2 teaspoons umeboshi plum vinegar

1 teaspoon wheat-free tamari

1 teaspoon agave syrup

Ground black pepper to taste

1. Place the torn kale leaves in a large bowl. Pour over 2 tablespoons of the olive oil and sprinkle with the ¼ teaspoon salt. Take off your rings and watch, roll up your sleeves and massage the oil and salt into the kale for 2 to 3 minutes, or until the kale starts to break down and wilt. Taste it to see if the kale's bitterness has gone. When it has, you can stop massaging.

2. Top the kale with the carrot, raisins, sesame and hemp seeds, and onion. Mix together with your hands.

3. In a small bowl, combine the lemon zest and juice, vinegar, 2 tablespoons of olive oil, tamari, agave, and salt and pepper. Stir well then toss with the salad, incorporating the dressing fully.

We prefer our salads lightly dressed, but if you like to go a bit heavy on the dressing, double the dressing ingredient quantities.

> **DID YOU KNOW?**
> Kale contains phytonutrients, which are anti-inflammatory, improve liver function and help to protect our brain cells from stress. Feeling frantic? Eat some kale!

WINTER SQUASH SALAD

We try to do the right thing for our health and the health of the planet. In that spirit, we encourage you to source raw, sustainable honey instead of reaching for the mass-produced versions. There are independent apiaries all over North America that are working to produce small batches of sustainable honey to help protect the bees. If you want to be strictly vegan, use agave syrup instead of raw honey in this recipe.

Active time: 20 minutes
Total time: 50 to 55 minutes
Makes 2 servings

1 medium butternut, buttercup or kabocha squash, or about 2 cups peeled, seeded and cubed squash

1 large red onion, diced

7 tablespoons olive oil

5 tablespoons balsamic vinegar

1 teaspoon dried rosemary

½ teaspoon dried thyme

1 teaspoon Dijon or stone-ground mustard

2 tablespoons raw sustainably-sourced honey or agave syrup

Pinch sea salt

3 cups arugula

2 cups mixed salad greens

4 tablespoons dried sweetened cranberries

4 tablespoons raw pumpkin seeds, toasted

2 tablespoons currants

1. Preheat the oven to 400°F. Line a baking sheet with parchment paper.

2. Peel and seed the squash, then cut it into 1-inch chunks. Place the squash and red onion in a large bowl and add 3 tablespoons of the olive oil, 1 tablespoon of the balsamic vinegar, rosemary and thyme. Toss to coat.

3. Transfer the squash mixture to the prepared baking sheet. Roast for 15 to 20 minutes, or until the squash has softened but isn't losing its shape. Set aside to cool for 15 minutes.

4. In a blender, on low speed, or using a whisk, combine the remaining 4 tablespoons of olive oil and 4 tablespoons of balsamic vinegar with the mustard, honey and salt. Set aside 3 tablespoons of this dressing.

5. In a large bowl, toss the cooled squash mixture with the remaining dressing.

6. Add the arugula, mixed greens and reserved dressing, and toss again to coat well.

7. Add the cranberries, pumpkin seeds and currants. Toss thoroughly one more time and serve.

To toast seeds, set a nonstick skillet over medium heat,
add the seeds and toast until they deepen in color and are fragrant.

MEGA SALAD

What is so wonderful about salads is the more you make them, the more you get comfortable with experimenting and discovering new favorite flavors. Trust us, salads are addictive. Treat this recipe as a guideline, substituting whatever nuts, seeds or sprouts are your faves.

Active time: 15 to 20 minutes

Total time: 15 to 20 minutes

Makes 4 servings

8 cups any greens (romaine, arugula and/or
    spinach), torn into bite-size pieces

2 cups any sprouts (radish, sunflower, pea,
    broccoli, lentil etc.)

1 cup fresh cilantro leaves, chopped

1 cup fresh basil leaves, chopped

1 cup fresh mint leaves, chopped

4 tablespoons fresh lime or lemon juice

¼ cup avocado oil

Pinch of sea salt

½ cup walnut pieces

½ cup dried blueberries

½ cup hemp seeds

½ cup raw sunflower seeds

¼ cup raw pumpkin seeds

2 avocados, pitted and cut into
    ½-inch chunks

2 tablespoons Brazil Nut "Parmesan"
    (page 96, optional)

1. In a large bowl, mix the greens, sprouts and herbs. Toss with lime juice.

2. Add the avocado oil and toss to coat the leaves thoroughly.

3. Sprinkle with salt to taste. Toss until well combined.

4. Add the walnuts, blueberries, hemp, sunflower and pumpkin seeds, and toss well.

5. Add the avocado chunks and toss gently to fully incorporate. Sprinkle with Brazil nut "Parmesan" (if using). Serve immediately.

Sprinkling the sea salt after the lime juice and avocado oil is an important step, as it helps the salt stick to the leaves and make the greens taste more fresh and vibrant.

BEST-EVER CAESAR SALAD

This is the salad that made Kindfood café famous, and possibly even put us on the map! We have had customers drive for hundreds of miles for it. Lettuce Love Café, of course, has the same salad with the same dressing (it's all about the dressing). For more adventurous souls, try the super easy variation, made with avocados, below. It'll make you feel like you're California Dreaming.

Active time: 15 minutes

Total time: 15 minutes

Makes 2 servings

6 tablespoons olive oil

4 tablespoons raw cashews

3 tablespoons fresh lemon juice

2 tablespoons wheat-free tamari

1 tablespoon stone-ground or Dijon mustard

1 tablespoon raw tahini

1 to 2 cloves garlic, minced (according
     to taste)

1 large head of romaine, removed from stalk

Gluten-free bread croutons

½ cup Brazil Nut "Parmesan"
     (page 96; optional)

1. Combine the oil, cashews, lemon juice, tamari, mustard, tahini, garlic and ¼ cup of filtered water in a food processor or blender. Process until well blended. Add another ¼ cup of filtered water to thin the dressing, if necessary, and process again until smooth.

2. In a large bowl, toss the romaine with the dressing to coat the leaves well.

3. Top with the croutons and a sprinkling of Brazil nut "Parmesan" (if using).

VARIATION:

Avocado Caesar Salad

1 cup roughly chopped avocado

½ cup raw cashews

2 tablespoons lemon juice

1 tablespoon olive oil

1 teaspoon minced garlic

1/2 teaspoon sea salt

1/2 teaspoon ground black pepper

¼ teaspoon chili flakes

6 cups of roughly torn romaine lettuce

1 cup of diced tomatoes

Handful of raw walnuts

½ cup Brazil Nut "Parmesan" (page 96, optional)

1. In a heavy-duty blender, blend the avocado, cashews, lemon juice, olive oil, garlic, salt, pepper, chili flakes and 1 cup of filtered water for about 1 minute or until smooth and creamy.

2. In a large bowl, toss the lettuce, tomatoes and walnuts with the dressing to coat the leaves well.

3. Serve sprinkled with Brazil nut "Parmesan" (if using).

Cumin-Scented Cornbread
(page 90)

Sides, Sauces & Condiments

CUMIN-SCENTED CORNBREAD (photo on page 88)

Your home will be filled with heavenly aromas while this cornbread bakes, making people flock to your kitchen because it's so difficult to wait. But try to be patient: the cornbread will crumble if you slice it before it has cooled slightly. This bread is an absolute must with the Tempeh Chili (page 65).

Active time: 10 minutes

Total time: 35 minutes

Makes 8 servings

Coconut oil or nonstick cooking spray

1 ½ cups cornmeal

1 cup gluten-free all-purpose flour

½ cup corn flour

1 tablespoon baking powder

2 teaspoons baking soda

¾ teaspoon xanthan gum

1 ½ teaspoons ground cumin

1 teaspoon ground coriander

1 teaspoon sea salt

½ teaspoon red chili flakes

4 tablespoons ground flax seed

1 cup unsweetened rice milk

1 teaspoon apple cider vinegar

1 cup plain unsweetened coconut milk yogurt or unsweetened almond milk yogurt

½ cup Sucanat

½ cup coconut oil, melted

2 teaspoons vanilla extract

1. Preheat the oven to 350°F. Lightly grease an 8-inch square cake pan, cornbread pan or 4 mini loaf pans with coconut oil or cooking spray.

2. In a medium bowl, whisk together the cornmeal, all-purpose flour, corn flour, baking powder, baking soda, xanthan gum, cumin, coriander, salt and chili flakes.

3. In a small bowl, mix the ground flax seed with ⅔ cup cold filtered water and set aside to thicken.

4. In a large bowl, combine the rice milk and vinegar and set aside for 5 minutes.

5. Add the yogurt, Sucanat, oil and vanilla to the rice milk mixture and whisk until combined.

6. Add the dry ingredients to the wet ingredients and stir very well. Add the flax mixture and stir again until fully combined.

7. Pour the batter into the prepared pan. Bake for 25 to 30 minutes, or until a tester inserted into the center of the cornbread comes out clean. Let the cornbread cool in the pan for 20 minutes before serving . . . if you can wait that long!

This is best eaten the day it's made but leftovers freeze beautifully.

SAVORY CHEESE BISCUITS

These are the perfect little nibble to go with our Creamy Butternut Squash Soup (page 74) or perhaps a glass of wine. The biscuits have a substantial texture because of the flax and a slightly decadent richness from the coconut oil. You'll find that you need to keep them out of sight but even so they won't last long!

Active time: 15 minutes
Total time: 30 to 35 minutes
Makes 24 biscuits

½ cup vegan butter

⅓ cup coconut oil, melted

⅓ cup applesauce

¼ cup Sucanat

1 teaspoon sea salt

2 cups gluten-free all-purpose flour

3 tablespoons nutritional yeast

2 teaspoons baking powder

1 teaspoon baking soda

1 teaspoon xanthan gum

1 tablespoon ground flax seed

1 tablespoon arrowroot starch

1 teaspoon dried oregano

1 teaspoon dried basil

1 teaspoon dried rosemary

½ teaspoon ground black pepper

Pinch of ground sage

1 cup shredded non-dairy cheddar-style
    cheese

Coarse sea salt to taste

1. Preheat the oven to 350°F. Line two baking sheets with parchment paper.

2. In a large bowl, combine the vegan butter, coconut oil, applesauce, Sucanat and salt.

3. In a medium bowl, mix the flour, nutritional yeast, baking powder, baking soda, xanthan gum, ground flax seed, arrowroot starch, oregano, basil, rosemary, pepper and sage.

4. Add the dry ingredients to the wet ingredients. Stir until well blended. Add the non-dairy cheddar and combine well. Feel free to use your hands to make sure everything is incorporated.

5. Divide the dough into 24 tablespoon-size pieces and shape into balls. Place 12 balls on each prepared baking sheet. Gently flatten each ball with the tines of a fork, making an X pattern. Sprinkle lightly with coarse salt.

6. Bake for 15 to 17 minutes, or until the biscuits are golden brown around the edges.

Coconut oil has a melting point of 76°F. If you leave the jar out on the countertop it will always be soft. To melt the oil to liquid form, fill a bowl with hot water and sit the jar in the water for a few minutes. We never use a microwave.

VEGGIE STUFFING

This has been a customer fave at the café since we've been in business. We love this stuffing any time of year and we're happy to share the recipe with anyone who asks. At holiday times, the requests can number in the thousands—it's that popular. Not only is it plant based, it's also gluten free, which is a win-win!

Active time: 20 minutes
Total time: 50 to 55 minutes
Makes 10 to 12 servings

11 cups gluten-free bread cubes

3 tablespoons olive oil

1 tablespoon vegan butter

1 ½ cups finely chopped celery

1 cup finely chopped yellow onion

1 tablespoon minced garlic

½ cup finely chopped fresh parsley

2 tablespoons minced fresh thyme

2 teaspoons dried sage

2 teaspoons dried thyme

½ teaspoon ground black pepper

Sea salt to taste

3 cups vegetable broth

1. Preheat the oven to 400°F. Lightly grease a 3-quart casserole dish that has a cover.

2. Spread the bread cubes out on a large baking sheet then bake until crisp and golden. Tip into a large bowl and set aside to cool.

3. In a large skillet, heat 2 tablespoons of the olive oil and the vegan butter over medium heat. Sauté the celery, onion and garlic for 3 minutes, or until soft.

4. Combine the sautéed veggies with the toasted croutons. Using your hands is the gentlest way to do this and give it love.

5. Stir in the parsley, fresh thyme, sage, dried thyme, pepper and salt. Drizzle with the remaining olive oil and stir well.

6. Add 2 cups of the veggie broth and mix gently until it has been absorbed.

7. Scrape the mixture into the prepared casserole dish. Cover and bake for 25 minutes. Uncover and return the dish to the oven for 5 to 10 more minutes, or until the top has browned.

BRAISED BRUSSELS SPROUTS

We keep hearing that people don't like Brussels sprouts, which usually means they don't like overcooked, soggy, strong-tasting vegetables by any name! We understand completely, which is why we eat our sprouts blanched, browned and braised in a savory mixture that's healthfully addictive.

Active time: 15 minutes
Total time: 25 minutes
Makes 4 servings

1 pound Brussels sprouts

¼ cup finely chopped pecans, pine nuts or walnuts

1 tablespoon olive oil

Pinch of sea salt

1 tablespoon thinly sliced shallots

2 cloves garlic, minced

2 tablespoons dry white wine or vegetable broth

1 teaspoon wheat-free tamari

¼ teaspoon sea salt

¼ teaspoon ground black pepper

1. Bring a large saucepan of water to a boil and fill a large bowl with ice water. Add the sprouts to the boiling water and cook for about 3 minutes, or until tender-crisp. Do not overcook!

2. Drain the sprouts and immediately plunge them into the ice water.

3. Meanwhile, toast the pecans in a very large cast iron skillet over medium heat for about 4 minutes, or until golden brown. Remove the pecans from the skillet and set aside.

4. In the same skillet, heat the olive oil and a sprinkle of salt over medium heat. Add the sprouts, cut sides down, and cook for about 5 minutes, or until the cut sides are browned.

5. Stir in shallots and garlic and cook for about 1 minute, or until fragrant and soft.

6. Stir the pecans into the hot sprouts. Add the wine, tamari, salt and pepper and cook, stirring for 1 minute to reduce the liquid. Serve immediately.

To prepare a cast iron skillet for frying, you can make it nonstick by rubbing it with olive oil, then sprinkling it with sea salt.

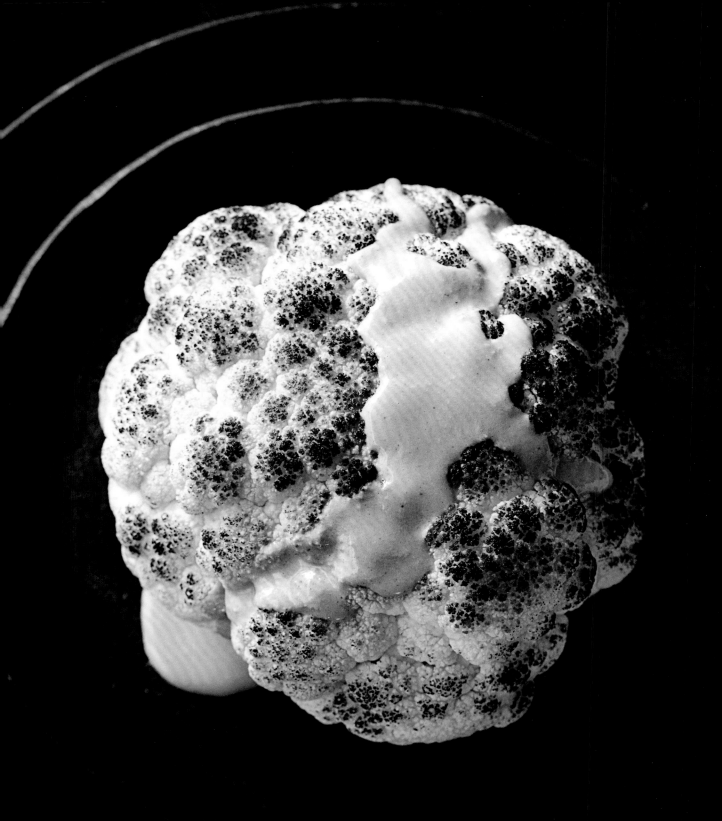

ROASTED CAULIFLOWER

This is an attention-getter! We like to place it in the center of the dinner table and invite our guests to serve themselves. Cauliflower develops a wonderfully nutty flavor when it's roasted, which makes this dish something special. If you want to increase the elegance factor, serve it at a dinner party topped with the sauce from the Fettuccine Alfredo recipe (page 69) or with Cashew Cream (page 101).

Active time: 15 minutes
Total time: 75 minutes
Makes 4 to 6 servings

2 ½ cups dry white wine or vegetable broth

⅓ cup olive oil

¼ teaspoon sea salt

3 tablespoons fresh lemon juice

2 tablespoons maple syrup

1 tablespoon red chili flakes

1 head cauliflower, left whole,
    outer leaves trimmed

3 tablespoons nutritional yeast

Olive oil to serve

Additional sea salt to serve

1. Preheat the oven to 475°F. Lightly oil a baking sheet or roasting pan.

2. In a large stockpot, bring 8 cups of filtered water, the wine, olive oil, salt, lemon juice, maple syrup and chili flakes to the boil.

3. Carefully lower the cauliflower into the boiling liquid. Reduce the heat and simmer, turning the cauliflower occasionally, for 15 to 20 minutes, or until a knife can be easily inserted into the cauliflower's stalk.

4. Using slotted spoons, gently transfer the cauliflower to a colander. Roll the drained cauliflower out of the colander and onto the prepared baking sheet.

5. Sprinkle the cauliflower with nutritional yeast and roast, rotating the pan after 20 minutes, for 30 to 40 minutes, or until the cauliflower is well browned.

6. Transfer the roasted cauliflower to a platter. Drizzle with a little olive oil and sprinkle with salt to taste. Serve as is or with the sauce of your choice (see note above).

> **DID YOU KNOW?**
> Cauliflower helps fight against cancer, boosts heart health and is anti-inflammatory. It's also rich in vitamins C, K and B$_6$, and protein. Cauliflower boosts brain health and even helps with digestion.

CHIPOTLE MASHED SWEET POTATOES

Mashed potatoes have a bad rap for being fat-laden heavyweights. Our version replaces the dairy products with healthy alternatives that won't slow you down. This mash tastes rich and creamy, and any leftovers can be used in all kinds of ways including on our savory pancakes (page 45)! The chipotle seasoning complements the sweet potatoes perfectly.

Active time: 5 to 10 minutes
Total time: 25 minutes
Makes 4 servings

6 medium sweet potatoes, peeled and cut
    into 1-inch pieces
½ cup thick Cashew Cream (page 101)
¼ cup vegan butter
¼ teaspoon chipotle chili powder
Sea salt to taste

1. In a saucepan of boiling water, cook the sweet potatoes for about 10 minutes, or until soft. Drain and return the sweet potatoes to the saucepan.
2. Add the cashew cream, vegan butter and chili powder. Mix thoroughly with an electric hand mixer or immersion blender, making the mash as lumpy or smooth as you like. Season with salt to taste.

BRAZIL NUT "PARMESAN"

This crumble makes a savory, tasty addition to many dishes, from salads to pasta to sandwiches. You will never miss Parmesan again. Brazil nuts are full of healthy fats that won't clog your arteries.

Active time: 5 to 8 minutes
Total time: 5 to 8 minutes
Makes 2 cups

2 cups Brazil nuts
½ cup nutritional yeast
1 large clove garlic, minced
¾ teaspoon sea salt

1. Pulse the Brazil nuts in a very dry food processor fitted with the metal blade until the nuts are evenly crumbled. Make sure there is no moisture in the processor or you will end up with Brazil nut butter.
2. Add the nutritional yeast, garlic and salt. Pulse two or three times to combine the garlic and salt with the nuts.
3. Pour the mixture into a glass storage container with a lid and use as needed. It will keep in the refrigerator for 7 to 10 days.

DID YOU KNOW?

Brazil nuts are the highest natural source of selenium, a mineral that helps prevent coronary artery disease, cirrhosis and some cancers. Just one or two nuts a day provide enough selenium to make a difference to your health.

MISO GRAVY

 This gravy is delicious on Nut, Quinoa & Millet Loaf (page 64), on simple red-skinned mashed potatoes or even poured over savory pancakes for dinner. Yum! Try to find non-GMO miso, if possible. The last thing you need is genetically modified weirdness in your diet when you're trying to eat in a healthful way.

Active time: 10 to 15 minutes

Total time: 10 to 15 minutes

Makes 1 ½ cups

4 ½ tablespoons white rice flour

¾ cup nutritional yeast

¼ teaspoon garlic powder

1 ½ cups vegetable broth or filtered water

⅓ cup extra virgin olive oil

3 tablespoons yellow miso paste

1 ½ teaspoons Dijon mustard

¾ teaspoon sea salt

Pinch of ground black pepper

1. In a medium saucepan over low heat, combine the rice flour, nutritional yeast and garlic powder. Whisk in the veggie broth to make a slurry. Bring to a boil and simmer for 30 seconds, whisking constantly, to cook out the raw, floury flavor.
2. Add the olive oil, miso paste, mustard, salt and pepper. Whisk until everything is incorporated and the mixture is smooth.
3. Serve hot. Reheat, if necessary, as this tastes best when hot.

We prefer the gentle, mellow flavor of yellow miso but if you want a deeper, richer taste, feel free to use brown miso. The result will look like a dark, mushroom-based gravy.

> **DID YOU KNOW?**
> Miso is high in B vitamins, especially B_{12}. It contains a phytochemical called genistein that some medical scientists believe can cut off blood flow to cancerous tumors, preventing them from growing. Miso also aids in digestion and restores probiotics to the intestines. Cook with miso!

SRIRACHA SAUCE

Most food-lovers have Sriracha sauce in their pantries these days, as it's great on just about everything. Here we share a souped-up version that's more complex and pourable, and a little sweeter than the sauce straight from the bottle. It's a must for our Cauliflower Wings (page 53).

Active time: 10 minutes
Total time: 10 minutes
Makes about 1 cup

½ cup prepared Sriracha sauce

¼ cup olive oil

¼ cup coconut oil, melted

1 tablespoon finely chopped onion

1 large clove garlic, minced

2 teaspoons maple syrup

1 teaspoon paprika

1 teaspoon rice vinegar

½ teaspoon Worcestershire sauce

¼ teaspoon cayenne pepper

1. In a blender, combine the Sriracha sauce, olive and coconut oils, onion, garlic, maple syrup, paprika, vinegar, Worcestershire sauce and cayenne. Blend until smooth.

2. Pour the sauce into a medium saucepan set over medium heat. Heat, whisking constantly, for about 5 minutes, or until bubbling. Remove from the heat and serve warm.

Refrigerate any unused sauce in a sealed container for up to two weeks.

TOMATO BASIL SAUCE

The secret to a fresh-tasting tomato sauce is to not overcook it. This sauce is versatile and freezes well.

Active time: 15 minutes
Total time: 40 minutes
Makes about 3 ½ cups, enough for 4 servings

2 tablespoons extra virgin olive oil

1 medium yellow onion, diced

1 small shallot, minced

2 cloves garlic, minced

1 can (28 ounces) diced tomatoes

1 teaspoon dried basil

¼ teaspoon sea salt

Ground black pepper to taste

¼ cup basil leaves, chopped

1. Heat the oil in a medium stockpot over medium-high heat and sauté the onion for 3 minutes, or until translucent. Add the shallots and garlic and sauté for 2 more minutes.

2. Stir in the tomatoes, dried basil and salt. Bring to a simmer then reduce the heat to low and simmer, uncovered, for 20 minutes. Stir in ¼ cup filtered water and simmer for 5 more minutes.

3. Remove from the heat. Transfer 3 cups of the sauce to a blender and blend, on high speed, until smooth and velvety. Pour the blended sauce back into the stock pot and stir to combine. Add the pepper and basil leaves and warm over medium heat for another minute or so.

HUMMUS

The steps to create deliciously perfect hummus are very important. The lemon juice and raw tahini set the stage and must be blended for at least two to three minutes. Because you really taste the olive oil in this recipe, use the best extra virgin oil you can afford—it will make all the difference. It's okay to use canned chickpeas, making the hummus quick and easy for anytime snacking. Serve this with crackers or raw vegetables, or use it as a spread for sandwiches.

Active time: 10 to 12 minutes
Total time: 10 to 12 minutes
Makes 2 cups

⅓ cup raw tahini

⅓ cup fresh lemon juice

1 tablespoon yellow miso paste

1 clove garlic, chopped

1 teaspoon sea salt

2 cups drained and rinsed canned chickpeas

¼ cup extra virgin olive oil

½ teaspoon ground cumin

½ teaspoon red chili flakes

Pinch of ground black pepper

Pinch of paprika for garnish

1. In a food processor, blend the tahini and lemon juice for about 2 to 3 minutes (the smoother the better).
2. Add the miso paste, garlic and salt, and process for one minute.
3. Add the chickpeas and olive oil and process until smooth.
4. Add the cumin, chili flakes and black pepper and process again.
5. If the hummus is too thick, add filtered water one tablespoon at a time and process until you achieve the desired consistency. Serve garnished with a sprinkle of paprika.

VARIATION:

Lime-Cumin Hummus

1. In step 1, substitute 4 tablespoons fresh lime juice and 3 tablespoons fresh lemon juice for the ⅓ cup lemon juice.
2. In step 4, increase the cumin to 1 teaspoon and add ½ teaspoon ground coriander.
3. Add 1 tablespoon chopped fresh cilantro to prepared hummus.

RANCH DRESSING

This is the perfect dipping sauce for our Cauliflower Wings (page 53) and is an awesome salad dressing.

Active time: 5 minutes
Total time: 5 minutes
Makes 1 ½ cups

¾ cup vegan mayonnaise

⅓ cup vegan sour cream

¼ cup vegan cream cheese

1 tablespoon lemon juice

1 teaspoon dried parsley

1 teaspoon dried dill

1 teaspoon garlic powder

1 teaspoon fresh parsley

1. In a blender, combine all the ingredients. Blend on high until smooth.

EGGLESS MAYO

For this mayo, pour the oil in gradually so that the mixture emulsifies instead of splitting or curdling. If your mayo separates after it has been refrigerated, a quick whisk should bring it back together. Adding a teaspoon of fresh lime juice to a cup of mayo will give you a wonderful lime *crema* that's delicious with Mexican recipes. Substitute this recipe for traditional mayo on almost anything.

Active Time: 5 to 10 min
Total time: 5 to 10 minutes
Makes 2 cups

½ cup unsweetened soy milk

1 tablespoon plus 1 teaspoon apple cider vinegar

1 tablespoon stone-ground mustard

1 tablespoon plus 1 teaspoon fresh lemon juice

1 teaspoon sea salt

1 ½ cups canola oil or olive oil

1. In a blender, combine the soy milk, vinegar, mustard, lemon juice and salt. Blend to combine.
2. With the motor running, slowly drizzle in the canola oil and continue to blend until the mixture has emulsified. When the mayo has emulsified completely, a spoon drawn through the mayo should create a trench that doesn't collapse.
3. Use as needed right away or refrigerate any unused mayo for up to 10 days.

VARIATION:

Chipotle Eggless Mayo

Mix ½ teaspoon chipotle chili powder into 1 cup of prepared eggless mayo.

CASHEW CREAM

This is a vegan staple that stands in for dairy in a variety of ways. In the raw food world, where it originated, it's used in lots of desserts, sauces and dressings. When you cook with it, though, it can replace so much more, from a cheese filling for ravioli to heavy cream in soups. Cashew cream reduces and thickens like dairy cream, which is not the case with all non-dairy milks.

Active time: 5 minutes

Total time: 35 minutes

Makes 2 ½ cups

2 cups raw cashews

1. Put the cashews in a bowl and add enough cold water to cover them. Cover the bowl and leave to soak for 30 minutes in the refrigerator.
2. Drain the cashews and rinse under cold water. Place in a heavy-duty blender with enough fresh filtered water to cover them by 1 inch.
3. Blend on high speed for several minutes until very smooth. For a thicker cream, add less water to the blender.

Cashew cream can be stored for 2 to 3 days in the fridge or frozen for up to 6 months (once defrosted it may need to go for a whirl in the blender).

Bake Shoppe Treats!

Raspberry-Coconut Bars (page 118).

Pies, Treats & Bars

GLUTEN-FREE PIE CRUST

Pastry is the most feared recipe in anyone's kitchen, and we're bringing you a dairy-, egg- and gluten-free version to boot! We hope to put your worries to rest and you will enjoy making this delicious variation on a classic. Kelly's great-aunt Laura always used apple cider vinegar—absolutely necessary for tender pastry— in her pie crust at the farm.

Active time: 20 minutes

Total time: 35 minutes

Makes one 9-inch single pie crust

⅓ cup millet flour

⅓ cup sorghum flour

⅓ cup brown rice flour or oat flour

⅓ cup arrowroot starch or tapioca starch

1 tablespoon organic cane sugar

½ teaspoon xanthan gum

1 teaspoon sea salt

½ cup palm shortening, chilled in the freezer
    for 15 minutes

1 teaspoon apple cider vinegar

1. Pour ½ cup of filtered ice water into a small bowl and set aside.

2. In a large bowl, whisk together the millet flour, sorghum flour, brown rice flour, arrowroot starch, sugar, xanthan gum and salt.

3. Tip the flour mixture into a food processor fitted with the metal blade, then add the palm shortening. Pulse until the shortening pieces are pea-size. Process the mixture for as little time as possible so the palm oil doesn't heat up and affect the consistency of the crust.

4. Tip the flour mixture back into the large bowl. Mix the vinegar with 2 tablespoons of the filtered ice water. Stir the vinegar mixture into the flour mixture. If the mixture does not clump together, add more filtered ice water, 1 teaspoonful at a time, stirring until the dough forms a ball.

5. Wrap the dough in plastic wrap and refrigerate for at least 15 minutes or up to 1 hour. The dough will be sticky; refrigerating it makes it easier to work with.

6. Place parchment paper on a rolling surface and sprinkle with rice flour. Generously flour the dough and roll out to a circle 12 inches in diameter.

7. Invert a 9-inch pie plate over the rolled dough, place your hand under the parchment paper and flip the pie plate upright. Peel off the parchment paper and press the dough onto the bottom and sides of the plate. If there are any tears, just use your fingers and a little filtered water to patch the pastry.

To prebake a pie crust before filling it, preheat the oven to 375°F. Prick the bottom of the pie crust multiple times with a fork. Line the crust with a circle of parchment paper and fill with dried beans to keep the crust flat. Bake for about 15 minutes, or until the crust is golden brown. Cool before filling.

RAW NUT PIE CRUST

Here's a no-fail crust that will work even when your oven is on the fritz. It couldn't be easier to pull together, and actually makes a great healthy snack all on its own when rolled into balls and frozen.

Active time: 15 minutes

Total time: 8 ¼ hours, including refrigerating time

Makes one 9-inch single pie crust

2 cups raw almonds

2 cups pitted dates

2 teaspoons vanilla extract

1 teaspoon sea salt

1. Soak the almonds in filtered water in the refrigerator for 8 hours or overnight. Drain. Rinse well and drain one more time.

2. Soak the dates for 30 minutes in warm filtered water to soften them.

3. Transfer the soaked almonds and dates to a food processor fitted with the metal blade. Add the vanilla and salt. Pulse just until combined.

4. Press the crust into the base of a 9-inch springform pan and freeze until ready to use.

FROZEN CHOCOLATE PIE

We've used soaked raw nuts elsewhere in this book, so you already know the milky richness that results from this important step. Here, the soaked cashews are a brilliant alternative to cream cheese or silken tofu, making this frozen chocolate pie gluten-free, soy-free, and completely raw. It's also completely delicious!

Active time: 10 minutes
Total time: 60 minutes
Makes one 9-inch pie

FOR THE FILLING:

1 frozen Raw Nut Pie Crust (page 107)

3 ½ cups raw cashews, soaked in
    filtered water for about 30 minutes
    then drained

1 cup raw cacao powder

¾ cup agave syrup

1 tablespoon vanilla extract

¾ cup coconut oil, melted

FOR THE TOPPING:

⅔ cup raw cacao powder

⅔ cup coconut oil, melted

6 tablespoons agave syrup

2 teaspoons vanilla extract

1. Prepare the raw nut pie crust in a 9-inch springform pan.

2. To make the filling, combine the cashews, cacao powder, agave syrup, vanilla extract and ¾ cup filtered water in a blender. Blend until smooth. Add the coconut oil and blend again. (You may need to scrape down the sides of the blender a couple of times during blending.)

3. Pour the chocolate filling into the frozen pie crust. Freeze until the filling is firm.

4. To make the chocolate topping, mix together the cacao powder, coconut oil, agave syrup and vanilla extract.

5. Pour the chocolate topping over the frozen chocolate pie filling. Return the pie to the freezer until completely frozen. When you're ready to serve, use a knife dipped in hot water to slice the pie.

THE BEST PUMPKIN PIE

For the richest, most luscious texture, you really must use only full-fat coconut cream; none of that "light" nonsense will work here! You don't need a top crust, so just use the Gluten-Free Pie Crust recipe on page 106.

Active time: 10 minutes

Total time: 65 to 70 minutes

Makes one 9-inch pie

1 Gluten-Free Pie Crust (page 106)

¼ cup maple syrup

2 tablespoons arrowroot starch

1 can (15 ounces) pumpkin purée

½ cup organic cane sugar

½ cup full-fat coconut cream

2 tablespoons vegan butter

1 tablespoon ground cinnamon

1 tablespoon vanilla extract

1 teaspoon ground ginger

½ teaspoon ground nutmeg

Pinch of ground allspice

Pinch of sea salt

1. Preheat the oven to 375°F. Prepare and prebake the pie crust (see page 106).

2. In a small bowl, combine the maple syrup and arrowroot starch.

3. In a large bowl and using an electric hand mixer, mix together the pumpkin, sugar, coconut cream, vegan butter, cinnamon, vanilla, ginger, nutmeg, allspice and salt.

4. Add the arrowroot mixture and mix again until fully combined.

5. Scoop the pumpkin filling into the baked pie crust and bake for 45 to 55 minutes, or until the filling is firm.

6. Remove the pie from the oven and let sit for 10 minutes before serving. We love serving this pie warm.

You can make the pumpkin pie filling ahead of time and refrigerate it for up to 4 days.

AVOCADO CHOCOLATE MOUSSE

Erinn is very proud of this recipe and likes to boast about its health benefits. Raw cacao is a superfood that's high in fiber with 400 times the antioxidants of cocoa; avocado is also high in fiber and rich in omega-3 fats. This is a mood-enhancing (or calming) dessert that's a great choice for Valentine's Day.

Active time: 10 minutes

Total time: 10 minutes

Makes 4 to 6 servings

3 cups pitted ripe avocado

½ to ¾ cup unsweetened almond milk

6 tablespoons raw cacao powder

4 tablespoons maple syrup

3 dates, pitted and softened

1 teaspoon maca powder (optional)

1. Combine the avocado, ½ cup almond milk, cacao powder, maple syrup, dates and maca powder (if using) in a blender. Blend for 30 seconds, scraping down the sides of the blender, if necessary. Don't blend too much, unless you want to make a smoothie!

2. If the mixture is too thick to blend, add another splash of almond milk. You can serve this right away or refrigerate it overnight.

For a spicy mousse, add ½ teaspoon cayenne pepper and ½ teaspoon ground cinnamon.

DID YOU KNOW?

Maca, a Peruvian root most commonly available in powder form, is said to increase energy and stamina, and boost mood levels.

GRANDMA'S APPLE CRUMBLE

Let's be honest: most people think the topping is the best part of a fruit crumble. The crunchy, sweet oat nuggets are really "the icing on the cake," right? It may surprise you to learn you get a richer, crisper crumble topping using vegan butter than the butter of our grandmas. It's also much better for you. We love this served warm, with a scoop of vegan vanilla or coconut milk ice cream.

Active time: 20 minutes

Total time: 70 minutes

Makes 10 to 12 servings

FOR THE FILLING:

12 apples, peeled, cored and sliced

½ cup coconut sugar

3 tablespoons chia seeds

1 tablespoon arrowroot starch

2 teaspoons ground cinnamon

½ teaspoon ground nutmeg

¼ teaspoon sea salt

3 tablespoons fresh lemon juice

FOR THE TOPPING:

2 cups gluten-free rolled oats

1 cup vegan butter

¾ cup gluten-free all-purpose flour

¾ cup organic cane sugar

½ cup roughly chopped raw almonds

3 tablespoons unsweetened shredded
    coconut (optional)

1 tablespoon vanilla extract

1 ½ teaspoons baking soda

1 teaspoon ground cinnamon

½ teaspoon sea salt

1. Preheat the oven to 375°F. Grease a 13- x 9-inch baking dish.

2. To make the filling, combine the apples, coconut sugar, chia seeds, arrowroot starch, cinnamon, nutmeg and salt in a large bowl. Add the lemon juice and mix well.

3. To make the topping, combine the oats, vegan butter, flour, sugar, almonds, coconut, vanilla, baking soda, cinnamon and salt in a medium bowl. (Using your hands for this works best.) Clusters, which will get brown and crunchy during baking, should form in the mix.

4. Put the apple mixture into the prepared baking dish. Sprinkle with the topping.

5. Cover the dish with foil, then poke several holes in the foil to allow the steam to escape.

6. Bake for 45 to 50 minutes. Remove the foil and "rake" the crumble with a fork. Return the crumble to the oven for 10 more minutes, or until the topping is golden brown. Allow the crumble to cool for 5 to 10 minutes before serving.

The crumble can be refrigerated for up to a week,
and leftovers make a yummy breakfast.

CHOCOLATE-PUMPKIN BREAD PUDDING

We love cinnamon-spiced pumpkin in just about any treat. Added to a luscious comfort food such as this chocolate-chip-spiked bread pudding, it reaches yummy new heights. It's almost over the top as is but becomes totally decadent topped with Salted Caramel Sauce (page 193) or Whipped Coconut Cream (page 196).

Active time: 15 minutes

Total time: 65 to 70 minutes

Makes 8 to 10 servings

Nonstick cooking spray

2 tablespoons ground flax seed

8 cups cubed day-old gluten-free bread
    (about 1 loaf)

4 cups vanilla coconut milk

1 can (15 ounces) pumpkin purée

¼ cup maple syrup

1 cup coconut sugar

⅔ cup vegan chocolate chips

¼ cup bourbon (optional)

3 tablespoons melted vegan butter

1 tablespoon vanilla extract

1 ½ teaspoons ground cinnamon

½ teaspoon sea salt

½ cup Salted Caramel Sauce (page 193)

1. Preheat the oven to 350°F. Lightly coat a baking sheet and a 13- x 9-inch baking dish with cooking spray.

2. Combine the ground flax seed with 6 tablespoons of filtered water and set aside to thicken.

3. Place the bread cubes on the prepared baking sheet. Bake for 10 to 15 minutes, or until lightly toasted. Transfer the toasted bread cubes to the prepared baking dish. Increase oven temperature to 375°F.

4. In a large bowl, stir together the coconut milk, pumpkin purée, coconut sugar, chocolate chips, bourbon (if using), vegan butter, vanilla, cinnamon, maple syrup and salt. Pour the mixture over the cubed bread, gently pushing the bread down to coat it evenly.

5. Cover the baking dish with foil and bake for 35 minutes. Poke several holes in the foil to allow steam to escape. Bake for 10 more minutes, or until the bread pudding has risen and is puffy.

6. Remove the bread pudding from the oven. Remove the foil and allow pudding to cool for 10 minutes before serving. Serve warm, cold or at room temperature, drizzled with caramel sauce.

GRANOLA BARS

❤️ Granola bars are good grab-and-go snacks but can be fat and sugar bombs without enough protein to see you through. These unbaked bars come together very easily; they are gluten- and dairy-free and have plenty of healthy protein, fiber and flavor to satisfy your snack attacks.

Active time: 25 minutes

Total time: 8 ½ hours, including refrigerating time

Makes 12 to 15 bars

3 cups gluten-free rolled oats

3 cups brown rice crisps

½ cup vegan chocolate chips or cacao nibs

½ cup raw almonds, roughly chopped

1 tablespoon chia seeds

½ teaspoon sea salt

1 ¾ cups raw almond butter

½ cup coconut oil

¼ cup coconut sugar

½ cup maple syrup

1 tablespoon vanilla extract

1 cup Chocolate Ganache
(page 192, optional)

1. Line the base of a 13- x 9-inch baking dish with parchment paper.

2. In a large bowl, mix together the oats, brown rice crisps, ¼ cup of the chocolate chips, the almonds, chia seeds, protein powder and salt.

3. In a medium saucepan, mix together the almond butter, coconut oil, coconut sugar, maple syrup and vanilla.

4. Heat over medium-low heat, stirring often, for 5 to 10 minutes, or until all the ingredients are fully incorporated. Remove from the heat and let cool.

5. Pour the cooled mixture over the oats mixture and stir to combine.

6. Press the mixture into the prepared dish and sprinkle with the remaining chocolate chips. Refrigerate for 8 hours or overnight. Cut into bars and serve, drizzled with chocolate ganache (if using).

These will keep well in the freezer for up to one month. If you want to make these bars extra healthy, use cacao nibs instead of chocolate chips. You can also substitute sunflower seed butter for almond butter to accommodate any nut allergies.

RASPBERRY-COCONUT BARS (photo on page 104)

These are so easy to whip up but people will think you fussed! You can use any cookies from your cupboard or freezer to blitz a batch of cookie crumbs in the food processor, so this recipe couldn't be simpler or more versatile. We encourage you to enjoy these with a glass of Chocolate Hemp Milk (page 24) for a chocolate-raspberry sensation.

Active time: 15 minutes

Total time: 40 minutes

Makes one 13- x 9-inch dish

5 cups cookie crumbs

6 tablespoons palm shortening, melted

4 tablespoons agave syrup

2 ¼ cups raspberry jam

2 cups unsweetened shredded coconut

1 cup gluten-free all-purpose flour

1 cup plus 1 tablespoon coconut oil, melted

Pinch of sea salt

1. Preheat the oven to 350°F. Line a 13- x 9-inch baking dish with parchment paper.

2. In a large bowl, combine the cookie crumbs with the melted palm shortening and agave syrup. Press firmly and evenly into the prepared dish.

3. Bake the crust for 8 minutes, or until firm. Let cool before adding the jam layer.

4. In a medium bowl, stir together the jam and coconut, making sure the coconut is evenly distributed. Spread the jam mixture over the cooled crust.

5. In another medium bowl, combine the flour, melted coconut oil and salt. Cover the jam-coconut layer completely with the flour layer.

6. Bake for 15 minutes, or until the topping is golden brown in places. Allow to cool for 1 minute before slicing into bars or squares of whatever size you like.

PEACH-BLUEBERRY CRUMBLE BARS

The flavors of peaches and blueberries evoke warm, easy days. Remember to freeze some extra fruits in season to enjoy during the winter when you want to remember what summer tastes like. There are some excellent commercially frozen organic fruits available now, so check out your favorite organic grocery store.

Active time: 25 to 35 minutes
Total time: about 1 ½ hours
Makes 24 bars

FOR THE BASE AND TOPPING:

1 tablespoon ground flax seed

3 cups gluten-free all-purpose flour

1 cup organic cane sugar

1 teaspoon baking powder

1 teaspoon baking soda

1 teaspoon xanthan gum

¼ teaspoon sea salt

1 cup vegan butter

½ cup gluten-free rolled oats

¼ cup Sucanat

FOR THE FILLING:

5 cups peeled, pitted sliced peaches
    (see sidebar)

1 cup blueberries

2 tablespoons fresh lemon juice

1 tablespoon vanilla extract

1 cup organic cane sugar

½ cup white rice flour

1 tablespoon arrowroot starch

½ teaspoon ground cinnamon

¼ teaspoon sea salt

Pinch of ground nutmeg

1. Preheat the oven to 375°F. Grease a 13- x 9-inch baking dish.

2. In a small bowl, combine the ground flax seed with 3 tablespoons of filtered water and set aside to thicken.

3. To make the base and topping, whisk together the flour, sugar, baking powder, baking soda, xanthan gum and salt in a large bowl.

4. Using a pastry blender, fork or two knives, cut in the vegan butter. Add the flax mixture and stir until the dough is crumbly. Don't overmix.

5. Press half of the dough lightly over the bottom of the prepared dish. Refrigerate while you make the topping and filling.

6. Add the rolled oats and Sucanat to the remaining dough in the bowl. Refrigerate while you make the filling.

7. To make the filling, place the peaches and blueberries in a large bowl. Sprinkle the fruit with the lemon juice and vanilla, and stir.

8. In a separate bowl, whisk together the sugar, rice flour, arrowroot starch, cinnamon, salt and nutmeg. Pour the flour mixture over the fruit and stir gently with a wooden spoon or spatula.

9. Pour the fruit mixture over the chilled dough base. Crumble the sweetened dough topping evenly over the fruit.

10. Bake for 35 minutes, or until bubbling and golden brown. Remove from the oven and let cool in the dish for 30 minutes before cutting into bars.

It's easier to peel peaches if you blanch them first.
Bring a large pot of water to a boil and turn off the heat.
Immerse the peaches in the hot water for 2 minutes.
When you remove the peaches from the water,
the skins will slip off easily.

DATE SQUARES

These wonderful, old-fashioned date squares conjure memories of bake sales and pot-luck dinners. Some people claim to have the recipe for the world's best date squares. These are usually blue-ribbon-award-winning variations passed down from expert home bakers, but we'll bet those contain mounds of white sugar, butter and several eggs. Ours, of course, don't, and we promise you won't miss a thing.

Active time: 25 minutes

Total time: 60 minutes

Makes 18 date squares

FOR THE FILLING:

4 cups Medjool dates, pitted and chopped

½ cup coconut sugar

Grated zest of 1 lemon

¼ cup fresh lemon juice

Pinch of sea salt

FOR THE CRUMBLE BASE AND TOPPING:

2 ½ cups gluten-free rolled oats

2 ¼ cups gluten-free all-purpose flour

1 ⅔ cups organic cane sugar

1 cup vegan butter

⅔ cup palm shortening

2 teaspoons vanilla extract

1 ¼ teaspoons baking soda

½ teaspoon sea salt

1. Preheat the oven to 350°F. Line a 13- x 9-inch baking dish with parchment paper.

2. To make the filling, combine the dates, coconut sugar, lemon zest and juice, salt and 2 cups of filtered water in a large saucepan. Bring to a simmer and cook for about 10 minutes, or until a paste forms. Set aside to cool.

3. To make the crumble base and topping, using an electric hand mixer, combine the oats, flour, sugar, vegan butter, palm shortening, vanilla, baking soda and salt in a medium bowl.

4. Press half of the crumble mixture into the prepared baking dish.

5. Spread the cooled date filling over the base. Sprinkle the remaining crumble mixture over the date filling, pressing it down gently into the date mixture.

6. Bake for 35 minutes, or until the topping is golden brown. Let cool in the dish, then cut into squares.

NANAIMO BARS (photo on page 121)

These triple-layer bars are always crowd-pleasers. Our no-bake method means they come together very easily. Be sure to check the ingredients of your custard powder; some contain dairy products. Our favorite brand is the classic Bird's Traditional Custard Powder, vegan since 1837, when Alfred Bird developed it for his wife as a dairy-free alternative to traditional English custard. Now, *that's* love!

Active time: 35 to 40 minutes
Total time: 35 to 40 minutes
Makes 20 bars

FOR THE COCOA-COCONUT BASE:

2 tablespoons ground flax seed

1 ¼ cups palm shortening

½ cup plus 2 tablespoons cocoa powder, sifted

½ cup organic cane sugar

¼ cup vegan butter

3 cups crushed gluten-free graham crackers

2 cups unsweetened shredded coconut

FOR THE VANILLA CUSTARD:

¼ cup vanilla custard powder

¼ cup full-fat coconut cream

2 teaspoons vanilla extract

½ cup palm shortening

½ cup vegan butter

4 cups powdered sugar, sifted

FOR THE CHOCOLATE GANACHE:

1 ½ cups vegan chocolate chips

6 tablespoons vegan butter

1. Line a 13- x 9-inch baking dish with parchment paper.

2. To make the cocoa-coconut base, combine the ground flax seed with 6 tablespoons of filtered water in a small bowl and set aside to thicken.

3. In a medium saucepan, heat the palm shortening, cocoa powder, sugar and vegan butter over medium-low heat, stirring until smooth.

4. Remove the saucepan from the heat and stir in the flax mixture. Add the crushed graham crackers and coconut.

5. Press the cocoa mixture evenly into the prepared dish. Chill in the freezer while you make the custard layer.

6. To make the vanilla custard layer, mix together the custard powder and coconut cream in a small bowl until smooth. Stir in vanilla.

7. In a medium bowl, beat the palm shortening and vegan butter with an electric hand mixer until smooth and creamy. Add the custard mixture and beat until well blended. Gradually add the powdered sugar and beat for 3 to 5 minutes, or until fluffy and smooth.

8. Spread the vanilla custard mixture evenly over the chilled cocoa-coconut layer and return the dish to the freezer while you make the next layer.

9. To make the chocolate ganache, melt the chocolate chips and vegan butter in a double boiler until smooth. Quickly spread the ganache evenly over the custard layer.

10. Chill in the freezer until really solid. Use a knife dipped in hot water to cut into bars. Refrigerate any uneaten bars for up to 3 days.

TEFF BROWNIES

Many people have never heard of the nutritious grain called teff. Kelly first tasted teff flour in the delicious Ethiopian flat bread *injera*. This recipe is the result of experimenting with homemade teff flour to create a perfectly balanced gluten-free brownie with just the right texture and taste. Teff flour is available in the health-food aisle of most grocery stores.

Active time: 15 minutes
Total time: 55 to 60 minutes
Makes 15 brownies

1 tablespoon chia seeds

½ cup coconut oil or canola oil

½ cup vegan chocolate chips

¾ cup Sucanat or coconut sugar

1 cup applesauce (or ½ cup applesauce and
     ½ cup mashed banana)

2 teaspoons balsamic vinegar

2 teaspoons vanilla extract

⅔ cup teff flour

½ cup tapioca starch or arrowroot starch

⅓ cup cocoa powder

¼ cup sorghum flour or garbanzo bean flour
     or brown rice flour

2 teaspoons baking powder

½ teaspoon baking soda

½ teaspoon xanthan gum

½ teaspoon sea salt

1. Preheat the oven to 350°F. Grease an 8-inch or 9-inch square baking pan. (Either size is fine but the smaller pan will yield thicker brownies.)

2. In a small bowl, combine the chia seeds with 3 tablespoons of filtered water and set aside for 5 minutes to thicken.

3. Melt the coconut oil and chocolate chips in a double boiler until smooth, about 5 minutes. Add the Sucanat and stir until combined. Remove from the heat.

4. In a large bowl, stir together the applesauce, balsamic vinegar and vanilla. Fold in the chia seed mixture. Stir in the melted chocolate mixture.

5. In a medium bowl, whisk together the teff flour, tapioca starch, cocoa powder, sorghum flour, baking powder, baking soda, xanthan gum and salt.

6. Add the dry ingredients to the wet ingredients and stir well with a spatula. Don't use an electric mixer because you don't want to incorporate any air bubbles.

7. Pour the batter into the prepared pan and spread evenly with a spatula. Bake for 18 to 22 minutes, or until the center of the brownies looks soft and the edges are beginning to brown. Don't overbake or you get a perfect chewy, gooey brownie. Let cool in the pan before cutting into squares.

> **DID YOU KNOW?**
> One of the smallest grains in the world, teff has been used in baking for 4,000 years. Teff is approximately 12 percent protein and high in calcium. One cup of cooked teff offers about 123 mg of calcium, which is comparable to ½ cup cooked spinach. Teff is also an excellent source of vitamin C, a micronutrient not commonly found in grains.

BITE-SIZE BROWNIES

Sometimes one bite is all you need when you want a treat. These are perfect little brownies to tuck into your lunch bag or serve with other delectables for afternoon tea. And just in case you didn't realize, brownies are 100-percent kid-friendly, and these are also magically nutritious.

Active time: 15 minutes
Total time: 45 minutes
Makes 36 to 40 mini brownies

Nonstick cooking spray

1 tablespoon ground flax seed

1 cup gluten-free all-purpose flour

½ cup cocoa powder

½ cup organic cane sugar

½ cup Sucanat

¼ cup potato starch

2 tablespoons arrowroot starch

2 teaspoons baking powder

1 teaspoon sea salt

½ teaspoon xanthan gum

¼ teaspoon baking soda

½ cup coconut oil or canola oil

½ cup applesauce

½ cup hot black coffee (you can use
    decaf coffee, chocolate almond milk or
    chocolate soy milk as alternatives)

2 tablespoons vanilla extract

¼ cup vegan chocolate chips

2 cups Chocolate Ganache
    (page 192, optional)

1. Preheat the oven to 350°F. Spray mini muffin pans with cooking spray or line with mini cupcake liners.

2. In a small bowl, combine the ground flax seed with 3 tablespoons of filtered water and set aside to thicken.

3. In a medium bowl, mix together the flour, cocoa powder, sugar, Sucanat, potato starch, arrowroot starch, baking powder, salt, xanthan gum and baking soda.

4. In a small bowl, combine the flax mixture, coconut oil, applesauce, hot coffee and vanilla. Stir until smooth. Using a rubber spatula, gently fold in the flax seed mixture until fully incorporated. Stir in the chocolate chips.

5. Using a small ice-cream scoop or tablespoon, scoop the batter into the prepared mini muffin cups.

6. Bake the brownies in the center of the oven for 10 minutes, or until they have firm edges and soft centers. Don't overbake!

7. Let the brownies cool a little in the pan for 10 minutes before serving; they are best served warm topped with chocolate ganache.

Store any uneaten brownies in a sealed container in the freezer
to keep them fresh, but not the fridge because that will
dry them out. We love frozen brownies!

SPICY RAW CACAO TRUFFLES

When our craving for chocolate hits, these truffles are the answer. The addition of chili powder and cayenne pepper makes these truffles multitaskers. Both spices have several health benefits, including vitamins A, B and C; they're a digestive aid, help balance cholesterol, and offer a metabolic boost and relief from migraine headache and other pain. Cayenne also helps rid the body of cold and flu symptoms. What a superstar snack!

Active time: 20 to 25 minutes
otal time: 2 ½ hours
Makes 18 truffles

1 ½ cups raw cashews

¾ teaspoon ground cinnamon

¼ teaspoon chili powder

¼ teaspoon cayenne pepper

¼ teaspoon sea salt

¾ cup plus 2 tablespoons raw cacao powder

½ cup cacao nibs

⅔ cup maple syrup or dark raw agave syrup

½ cup coconut butter, softened

2 teaspoons vanilla extract

1. In a clean coffee grinder (see sidebar), grind the cashews, in small batches, until they are reduced to a fine powder.

2. Transfer the powdered cashews to a medium bowl. Stir in the cinnamon, chili powder, cayenne and salt. Stir in ¾ cup of the cacao powder and the cacao nibs.

3. Add the maple syrup and coconut butter. Stir with a wooden spoon at first, then use your hands to mix thoroughly. Add the vanilla and mix again with your hands.

4. Roll the truffle mixture into 1-inch balls, then roll the balls in the remaining cacao powder. Put the coated truffles in a single layer on a baking sheet.

5. Freeze the truffles for 2 hours. Eat one whenever you feel like a healthy pick-me-up. You can keep them at room temperature but they really are delicious kept in the freezer and eaten cold and firm.

A coffee grinder works better than a blender to grind nuts into a fine powder. An easy way to clean your grinder is to put a tablespoon of uncooked white rice in it. Grind the rice, shake it out of the grinder and *voilà*! the residue from coffee grounds will be gone.

Chocolate Cake (page 142)

Cupcakes, Cakes & Donuts

VANILLA CUPCAKES

This is one treat that no one will refuse. Delicate cupcakes that are rich and simply classic. One of our customers calls these "cupcakes without guilt" and "the best gluten-free cupcakes ever!" We think they're the best cupcakes. Period. And the same batter makes a wonderful vanilla layer cake.

Active time: 15 minutes

Total time: 35 to 40 minutes

Makes 24 cupcakes or one 8-inch double layer cake

3 cups gluten-free all-purpose flour

1 ½ teaspoons baking soda

1 ½ teaspoons baking powder

1 teaspoon sea salt

¾ teaspoon xanthan gum

¾ cup palm shortening

2 cups vanilla coconut milk yogurt

1 ½ cups organic cane sugar

1 tablespoon egg replacer (see page 153) plus ½ cup filtered water

1 tablespoon vanilla extract

4 cups Vanilla Buttercream Frosting (page 188)

Sparkling Sugar (we use India Tree) for sprinkling (optional)

1. Preheat the oven to 350°F. Line two 12-cup cupcake pans with paper liners, or grease two 8-inch cake pans.

2. In a medium bowl, whisk together the flour, baking soda, baking powder, salt and xanthan gum.

3. In a large bowl, cream the shortening, then add the yogurt, sugar, egg replacer mixture and vanilla. Beat until light and fluffy.

4. Add the dry ingredients to the wet ingredients and beat with an electric hand mixer.

5. Using an ice-cream scoop, divide the batter among the cupcake liners, or spoon into the cake pans, dividing evenly. Bake on the center rack for 18 to 20 minutes for cupcakes, 22 to 24 minutes for cake, rotating pans halfway through baking, until a cake tester inserted into the center of a cupcake or cake comes out clean.

6. Allow the cupcakes or cakes to cool completely on a wire rack before frosting with vanilla buttercream frosting or another frosting of your choice. Sprinkle each cupcake with Sparkling Sugar (if using).

MEXICAN CUPCAKES

We love a cupcake with some heat in it! The combination of cayenne, cinnamon and chocolate is decadent and addictive. The vanilla buttercream in the center cools the heat radiating from the cupcakes and the ganache enhances the deep, dark chocolate flavor.

Active time: 30 minutes
Total time: 65 minutes
Makes 12 cupcakes

1 cup minus 2 tablespoons gluten-free
    all-purpose flour
½ cup organic cane sugar
⅓ cup cocoa powder
¼ cup arrowroot starch
⅓ cup Sucanat
1 teaspoon baking powder
¾ teaspoon baking soda
½ teaspoon sea salt
¼ teaspoon xanthan gum
½ teaspoon ground cinnamon
⅛ teaspoon cayenne pepper
1 tablespoon ground flax seed
⅓ cup melted vegan butter or canola oil
2 tablespoons applesauce
¼ cup coconut or almond milk
⅓ cup sweet potato purée
1 tablespoon balsamic vinegar
1 teaspoon vanilla extract
2 cups Vanilla Buttercream Frosting
    (page 188)
1 cup Chocolate Ganache (page 192)

1. Preheat the oven to 350°F. Line a 12-cup cupcake pan with paper liners.

2. In a medium bowl, whisk together the flour, sugar, cocoa powder, arrowroot starch, Sucanat, baking powder, baking soda, salt, xanthan gum, cinnamon and cayenne until combined.

3. In a small bowl, combine the ground flax seed and 3 tablespoons of filtered water. Let sit for 3 minutes to thicken.

4. In a large bowl, combine the oil, applesauce, coconut milk, sweet potato purée, balsamic vinegar and vanilla and beat with an electric hand mixer on high for 1 minute.

5. Add the dry ingredients to wet ingredients and mix with an electric hand mixer until combined.

6. Using an ice-cream scoop, divide the batter among the cupcake liners. Bake on the center rack for 18 to 20 minutes or until a cake tester inserted into the center of a cupcake comes out clean. Do not overbake. Let the cupcakes cool completely on a wire rack.

7. Hollow out the center of each cupcake with a sharp knife, trying to retain a neat "cone" shape (you'll be placing the cutouts on top of the frosted cupcakes). Fill the hollow centers with vanilla buttercream frosting.

8. Freeze the cupcakes for 5 to 10 minutes to set the frosting.

9. Spoon chocolate ganache over the frozen vanilla frosting, then spread it to the edge of the liners. Top each cupcake with the reserved cutouts and you're ready to serve!

> **DID YOU KNOW?**
> The Ancient Mayans might have been the world's first chocoholics—beating us by more than 2,500 years! In their culture, cacao beans were a sacred superfood, reserved for royalty and the elite. Cacao was dried or roasted, then ground and served in numerous foods and drinks, often as a digestive aid.

PUMPKIN CUPCAKES

These cupcakes will warm you up from the inside. Ginger and cinnamon are natural metabolism boosters, which some people believe can help our bodies burn fat. We love to make these cupcakes after a long walk in the woods on a cool autumn afternoon.

Active time: 18 minutes

Total time: 70 to 80 minutes

Makes 12 cupcakes

2 tablespoons ground flax seed

1 ¾ cups gluten-free all-purpose flour

1 cup Sucanat

½ cup organic cane sugar

1 teaspoon baking powder

1 teaspoon baking soda

1 teaspoon ground ginger

1 teaspoon ground cinnamon

½ teaspoon xanthan gum

½ teaspoon sea salt

¼ teaspoon ground nutmeg

1 ½ cups canned pumpkin purée

½ cup coconut oil, melted

1 tablespoon vanilla extract

2 cups Cream Cheese Frosting (page 190)

½ cup Caramel Drizzle (page 193)

1. Preheat the oven to 350°F. Line a 12-cup cupcake pan with paper liners.

2. In a small bowl, combine the ground flax seed with 6 tablespoons of filtered water and set aside to thicken.

3. In a large bowl, whisk together the flour, Sucanat, sugar, baking powder, baking soda, ginger, cinnamon, xanthan gum, salt and nutmeg.

4. In a large bowl, combine the flax seed mixture with the pumpkin, coconut oil and vanilla and mix well. Add to the dry ingredients mixture. Combine with an electric hand mixer on medium-high speed.

5. Using an ice-cream scoop, divide the batter among the cupcake liners, filling them almost to the top. Bake for 22 to 25 minutes, or until a cake tester inserted into the center of a cupcake comes out clean. Do not overbake. Let the cupcakes cool completely on a wire rack before frosting with cream cheese frosting, and topping with our caramel drizzle.

RED VELVET CUPCAKES

Red velvet cupcakes have been around for decades. During the Second World War, when foods were rationed, bakers used boiled beets to enhance the flavor and color of their baked goods. At Kelly's Bake Shoppe, we use beet juice to make our cakes and cupcakes a beautiful rich red. Beets give a natural sweetness to baked goods, too, so you can cut back on the sugar.

Active time: 20 minutes

Total time: 30 to 40 minutes

Makes 12 cupcakes

1 ¾ cups organic cane sugar

1 cup white rice flour

1 cup garbanzo and fava flour blend

¾ cup arrowroot starch

2 tablespoons cocoa powder

1 teaspoon baking powder

1 teaspoon baking soda

1 teaspoon xanthan gum

1 teaspoon sea salt

1 cup rice milk

⅔ cup canola oil

½ cup beet juice

2 teaspoons vanilla extract

2 cups Vanilla Buttercream Frosting,
    tinted pink (page 188)

1. Preheat the oven to 350°F. Line a 12-cup cupcake pan with paper liners.
2. In a medium bowl, whisk together the sugar, rice flour, flour blend, arrowroot starch, cocoa powder, baking powder, baking soda, xanthan gum and salt.
3. In a large bowl, combine the rice milk, canola oil, beet juice and vanilla. Add the dry ingredients to the wet ingredients and mix with an electric hand mixer.
4. Using an ice-cream scoop, divide the batter among the cupcake liners, filling them three-quarters full.
5. Bake on the center rack for 20 to 22 minutes, or until a cake tester inserted into the center of a cupcake comes out clean. Do not overbake. Let the cupcakes cool completely on a wire rack before frosting with vanilla buttercream frosting.

This batter is really great after it's been refrigerated for a few hours.
Any leftover batter will keep in the fridge for up to 3 days.

DID YOU KNOW?

There are chemical food dyes in widespread use, many of which have been found to be toxic, even carcinogenic. Red food coloring is the worst of these. We avoid it always because it's petroleum-based and indigestible. It's known to adversely affect metabolism and brain function (especially in children's developing brains). Instead we use beet juice to colour ours a beautiful pink colour (see page 188).

CHOCOLATE SNOWBALL CUPCAKES

💙 These cupcakes always sell out quickly at the bakery. Who doesn't love a chocolate cupcake? And when it's topped with a snowfall of shredded coconut, well, it's all the more fun. Kelly says these are reminiscent of a Bounty bar, her favorite chocolate craving as a kid.

Active time: 10 minutes
Total time: 35 minutes
Makes 12 cupcakes

1 tablespoon ground flax seed

⅞ cup gluten-free all-purpose flour

½ cup organic cane sugar

⅓ cup cocoa powder

¼ cup arrowroot starch

⅓ cup Sucanat

1 teaspoon baking powder

¾ teaspoon baking soda

½ teaspoon sea salt

⅓ teaspoon xanthan gum

⅓ cup melted vegan butter or canola oil

⅓ cup sweet potato purée

2 tablespoons applesauce

⅓ cup coconut milk

1 teaspoon vanilla extract

1 teaspoon natural coconut extract

¼ cup unsweetened shredded coconut,
    plus 1 cup for topping

2 cups Vanilla Buttercream Frosting
    (page 188)

1. Preheat the oven to 350°F. Line a 12-cup cupcake pan with paper liners.

2. In a small bowl, combine the ground flax seed with 3 tablespoons filtered water and set aside to thicken.

3. In a medium bowl, whisk together the flour, sugar, cocoa powder, arrowroot starch, Sucanat, baking powder, baking soda, salt and xanthan gum until combined.

4. In a large bowl, combine the melted vegan butter, sweet potato purée, applesauce, vanilla and coconut extract. Add the flax mixture. Stir.

5. Add the dry ingredients to the wet ingredients and mix with an electric hand mixer until combined. Mix in ½ cup of the shredded coconut and continue to beat for for 30 seconds.

6. Using an ice-cream scoop, divide the batter among the cupcake liners. Bake on the center rack for 18 to 20 minutes, or until a cake tester inserted into the center of a cupcake comes out clean. Do not overbake. Let the cupcakes cool completely on a wire rack before topping each with a dollop of vanilla buttercream frosting.

7. Transfer the remaining shredded coconut to a small bowl. One at a time, roll the frosted cupcake tops in the coconut, pressing down gently to coat the tops completely.

DULCE DE LECHE CUPCAKES

These are our scrumptious, award-winning cupcakes. With them, we have won Best in Show at the Toronto Vegan Bake-Off and Best Cupcake in Burlington three years in a row! Filled with our homemade caramel sauce, they're so moist and delicious, one taste and you'll know why we took home the Grand Prize.

Active time: 25 minutes

Total time: 45 to 50 minutes

Makes 24 cupcakes

3 cups gluten-free all-purpose flour

1 ½ teaspoons baking soda

1 ½ teaspoons baking powder

1 teaspoon sea salt

¾ teaspoon xanthan gum

2 cups vanilla coconut milk yogurt

1 tablespoon fresh lemon juice

½ cup vegan shortening

¼ cup canola oil

1 cup organic cane sugar

¾ cup coconut milk

½ cup Sucanat

1 tablespoon arrowroot starch

1 tablespoon vanilla extract

½ cup Salted Caramel Sauce (page 193)

4 cups Vanilla Buttercream Frosting

    (page 188)

1. Preheat the oven to 350°F. Line two 12-cup cupcake pans with paper liners.

2. In a medium bowl, whisk together the flour, baking soda, baking powder, salt and xanthan gum. Set aside.

3. In a small bowl, combine the yogurt and lemon juice. Set aside.

4. In a large bowl, cream the shortening and oil with an electric hand mixer. Add the sugar, coconut milk, Sucanat, arrowroot starch and vanilla. Beat for 2 minutes, or until light and fluffy.

5. Add the dry ingredients to the shortening mixture in three batches, alternating with the yogurt and ending with the flour mixture.

6. Using an ice-cream scoop, divide the batter among the cupcake liners. Bake on the center rack for 18 to 20 minutes, or until a cake tester inserted into the center of a cupcake comes out clean. Do not overbake. Let the cupcakes cool completely on a wire rack.

7. Use a wooden skewer to poke a hole in the middle of each cupcake and drizzle in about 1 tablespoon of the salted caramel sauce.

8. Using a piping bag or by hand, frost the cupcakes with vanilla buttercream frosting. Drizzle a little more salted caramel sauce over the top of each.

CHOCOLATE CAKE (photo on page 128)

❤ This is the best chocolate cake you'll ever eat. Seriously. It's so moist, delicious and rich, you'll want to have it for breakfast, lunch and dinner. The same batter also makes absolutely classic chocolate cupcakes, perfect for parties or special occasions when only chocolate will do the trick.

Active time: 15 minutes
Total time: 35 minutes
Makes 36 cupcakes or one 8-inch
  triple–layer cake

2 ½ cups plus 1 tablespoon gluten-free
    all-purpose flour
1 ½ cup organic cane sugar
1 cup cocoa powder
¾ cup arrowroot starch
1 cup Sucanat
1 tablespoon baking powder
2 ½ teaspoons baking soda
1 ½ teaspoons sea salt
1 teaspoon xanthan gum
3 tablespoons ground flax seed
1 cup melted vegan butter or canola oil
⅓ cup applesauce
1 cup coconut or almond milk
1 cup sweet potato purée
1 tablespoon vanilla extract
6 cups Chocolate Buttercream Frosting
    (page 188)

1. Preheat the oven to 350°F. Grease three 8-inch cake pans or line 36 cupcake cups with paper liners.
2. In a medium bowl, whisk together the flour, sugar, cocoa powder, arrowroot starch, Sucanat, baking powder, baking soda, salt and xanthan gum until combined.
3. In a small bowl, combine the ground flax seed with ⅔ cup filtered water and set aside to thicken.
4. In a large bowl, combine the melted vegan butter, applesauce, coconut milk, sweet potato purée and vanilla with a hand mixer and beat for 1 minute on high. Add the flax mixture and continue to beat for another minute.
5. Add the dry ingredients to the wet ingredients and mix with an electric hand mixer until combined.
6. Divide the batter between the prepared cake pans or scoop into the cupcake liners.
7. Bake on the center rack for 22 to 24 minutes for the cakes, 18 to 20 minutes for the cupcakes, or until a cake tester inserted into the center of the cakes or cupcakes comes out clean.
8. Allow the cakes or cupcakes to cool completely on a wire rack before frosting with chocolate buttercream frosting or another frosting of your choice.

CARROT CAKE

We have always had a sweet spot for carrot cake. We created this one without any eggs, wheat or gluten in it and we wanted to make sure it was moist and full of flavor. Pineapple and coconut help to boost the natural sweetness of carrots and they also enhance the grated carrot in the cake to produce a really nice texture. We love this cake!

Active time: 25 minutes

Total time: 40 to 50 minutes

Makes one 9-inch triple-layer cake

Nonstick cooking spray (optional)

3 ½ cups gluten-free all-purpose flour

1 tablespoon baking powder

2 teaspoons baking soda

1 ½ teaspoons xanthan gum

1 ½ teaspoons ground cinnamon

1 teaspoon sea salt

1 teaspoon ground ginger

¼ teaspoon ground allspice

1 ¼ cups coconut milk

1 teaspoon apple cider vinegar

2 cups Sucanat

1 ¼ cups canola oil or melted coconut oil

¼ cup maple syrup

2 teaspoons vanilla extract

3 ½ cups grated carrot

½ cup raisins

¼ cup unsweetened shredded coconut

¼ cup drained canned pineapple pieces

6 cups Cream Cheese Frosting (page 190)

1. Preheat the oven to 350°F. Lightly grease three 9-inch cake pans with cooking spray or line with parchment paper.

2. In a medium bowl, whisk together the flour, baking powder, baking soda, xanthan gum, cinnamon, salt, ginger and allspice. Set aside.

3. In a small bowl, combine the coconut milk and vinegar. Set aside.

4. In a large bowl and using an electric hand mixer, combine the Sucanat, oil, maple syrup and vanilla. Add the coconut milk mixture and mix again briefly.

5. Add the dry ingredients to the wet ingredients. With the mixer, mix until the ingredients are combined and beginning to thicken.

6. Stir in ¼ cup of hot filtered water. Fold in the carrot, raisins, coconut and pineapple.

7. Pour the cake batter into the prepared pans, dividing evenly. Bake on the center rack for 20 to 25 minutes, or until a cake tester inserted in the center of the cakes comes out clean.

8. Allow to cool completely on a wire rack before frosting with cream cheese frosting.

LEMON POPPY SEED LOAF

Moist and luscious, this is the perfect lemon loaf to accompany a cup of afternoon tea. Be sure to let the loaf cool completely before you drizzle over the glaze. Otherwise, it will be absorbed completely and you'll miss out on the sweet-tart surprise.

Active time: 20 minutes
Total time: 60 to 70 minutes
Makes one 9- x 5-inch loaf

1 tablespoon ground flax seed

1 tablespoon chia seeds

2 cups gluten-free all-purpose flour

¾ cup organic cane sugar

¼ cup Sucanat

3 tablespoons poppy seeds

1 tablespoon baking powder

1 teaspoon baking soda

1 teaspoon xanthan gum

¾ teaspoon sea salt

1 cup almond or rice milk

1 tablespoon finely grated lemon zest

1 tablespoon fresh lemon juice

2 teaspoons natural lemon extract

1 teaspoon vanilla extract

½ cup melted vegan butter

Lemon Glaze (page 194)

1. Preheat the oven to 350°F. Lightly grease a 9- x 5-inch loaf pan.

2. In a small bowl, combine the ground flax seed and chia seeds with 6 tablespoons of filtered water and set aside to thicken.

3. In large bowl, whisk together the flour, sugar, Sucanat, poppy seeds, baking powder, baking soda, xanthan gum and salt.

4. In a medium bowl, combine the flax and chia mixture, milk, lemon zest and juice, lemon extract and vanilla.

5. Add the wet ingredients to the dry ingredients and mix well with an electric hand mixer. Gently fold in the melted butter.

6. Scoop the batter into the prepared loaf pan. Bake on the center rack for 50 minutes, rotating the pan after 25 minutes, until golden brown and a cake tester inserted in the center of the loaf comes out clean.

7. Let the loaf cool completely in the pan before removing to a wire rack.

8. Use a small spoon to drizzle the lemon glaze over the cooled loaf. Let the glaze soak in for a few minutes before serving.

BANANA-BUTTERSCOTCH LOAF

No banana should ever be wasted! For this recipe, the very ripest, black-skinned bananas are the best. They have a delicious, almost rum-flavored note that unripe bananas don't have. Always peel and chop bananas into chunks before putting them into freezer bags to use later in smoothies and, of course, banana bread.

Active time: 15 minutes
Total time: 70 minutes
Makes 6 to 8 mini loaves

Nonstick cooking spray

1 ¼ cups brown rice flour

1 cup gluten-free all-purpose flour

2 teaspoons baking powder

½ teaspoon baking soda

½ teaspoon xanthan gum

½ teaspoon sea salt

½ cup coconut or almond milk

1 teaspoon apple cider vinegar

½ cup vanilla coconut milk yogurt

⅔ cup Sucanat

½ cup organic cane sugar

⅔ cup coconut oil, melted

½ cup maple syrup

1 teaspoon vanilla extract

5 large ripe bananas, peeled and mashed
    (about 2 cups)

½ cup Caramel Drizzle (page 193)

1. Preheat the oven to 350°F. Spray 6 to 8 mini loaf pans with cooking spray.

2. In a large bowl, sift together the rice flour, all-purpose flour, baking powder, baking soda, xanthan gum and salt. Set aside.

3. In a small bowl, combine the almond milk and vinegar. Set aside.

4. In a medium bowl, combine the yogurt and almond milk mixture. Beat in the Sucanat, sugar, coconut oil, maple syrup and vanilla. Stir in the mashed bananas, just to combine.

5. Half-fill each mini loaf pan with batter. Spoon some caramel drizzle down the center of each loaf and top with the remaining batter. Bake on the center rack for 20 to 22 minutes or until a toothpick inserted in the center of a loaf comes out clean.

6. Allow to cool in the pans for 10 minutes. Remove and serve warm with additional caramel drizzle, if you wish.

KEY LIME CHEESECAKE

This no-bake beauty features only raw ingredients, and that includes the crust! It's the perfect summer dessert. Key limes are available all year but you can be sure to find them from June to August, when they are at their peak growing season in south Florida. You can use regular limes but the flavor won't be as complex. This cheesecake looks lovely sprinkled with extra lime zest or shredded coconut.

Active time: 15 minutes

Total time: 4 ¼ hours

Makes one 9-inch cheesecake

1 frozen Raw Nut Pie Crust (page 107)

4 cups raw cashews, soaked in filtered water for about 30 minutes then drained

¾ cup agave syrup or maple syrup

6 tablespoons finely grated key lime zest

⅔ cup fresh key lime juice

Pinch of sea salt

¾ cup melted coconut oil

1 frozen Raw Nut Pie Crust (page 107)

1. Prepare the raw nut pie crust in a 9-inch springform pan.

2. In a blender, blend the cashews, agave syrup, lime zest and juice and salt until smooth. Add the coconut oil and blend again, scraping down the sides of the blender as necessary.

3. Spoon the key lime filling into the frozen pie crust. Freeze for about 4 hours, or until the filling is frozen solid.

SALTED CARAMEL CHEESECAKE

Have you noticed that salted caramel is everywhere these days? In sweet and savory foods, on fine-dining menus and even in your favorite fancy coffee? Well, if you haven't tried it yet, get ready for your next flavor addiction. This no-bake cheesecake makes it easy to indulge. You can thank us later.

Active time: 30 minutes
Total time: 4 hours, including freezing time
Makes 12 servings

1 frozen Raw Nut Pie Crust (page 107)

4 ½ cups raw cashews, soaked in filtered water for about 30 minutes then drained

1 cup agave syrup

½ cup fresh lemon juice

1 tablespoon vanilla extract

¾ teaspoon sea salt

1 ¼ cups melted coconut oil

1 cup Caramel Drizzle (page 193)

1. Prepare the raw nut pie crust in a 9-inch springform pan.

2. In a heavy-duty blender, blend the cashews, agave syrup, lemon juice, vanilla and salt for about 3 minutes, or until smooth. Add the coconut oil and blend again, scraping down the sides of the blender as necessary.

3. Pour the cheesecake mixture into the frozen pie crust and smooth the surface. Freeze for about 3 hours, or until firm.

4. Spoon the caramel drizzle over the frozen cheesecake. Cut into 1-inch slices for serving. The servings are dainty because this cheesecake is super rich and filling.

Soaking the cashews makes it easier to blend them smoothly. We soak ours for about 30 minutes.

PUMPKIN CHEESECAKE

Nothing says "Thanksgiving" like a pumpkin cheesecake, especially our version. We created this rich, creamy and delicious recipe back in the Kindfood café days (circa 2010), and our customers have loved it ever since. It's definitely one of our go-to recipes for entertaining at home, too.

Active time: 20 minutes

Total time: 2 ¾ hours

Makes one 8-inch cheesecake

FOR THE COOKIE BASE:

2 ½ cups World Peace Cookie crumbs
      (page 160)

3 tablespoons coconut oil, melted

FOR THE PUMPKIN FILLING:

3 tablespoons egg replacer (see sidebar)

16 ounces vegan cream cheese (must be
      soy-based, we like Tofutti or Yoso)

⅔ cup Sucanat

4 tablespoons maple syrup

½ cup canned pumpkin purée

1 teaspoon ground ginger

½ teaspoon ground nutmeg

Pinch of ground cinnamon

Pinch of ground allspice

Pinch of sea salt

Whipped Coconut Cream (page 196)
      to serve

1. Preheat the oven to 400°F. Lightly grease an 8-inch springform pan.

2. To make the cookie base, combine the cookie crumbs and oil in a medium bowl, until the mixture clumps together. Press over the base of the prepared pan. Bake for 7 minutes or until the base hardens slightly.

3. To make the pumpkin filling, whisk together the egg replacer and 2 tablespoons of hot filtered water in a small bowl. Set aside for 3 to 5 minutes to thicken.

4. In a medium bowl and using an electric hand mixer on medium speed, cream the cream cheese with the Sucanat and maple syrup until fluffy. Add the egg replacer, pumpkin purée, ginger, nutmeg, cinnamon, allspice and salt. Mix until combined.

5. Pour the pumpkin filling over the cooled base. Bake for 8 minutes then reduce the oven temperature to 275°F. Bake for 50 to 60 minutes, until the cheesecake is firm around the edges but still soft and jiggly in the middle.

6. Immediately after removing the cake from the oven, run a sharp knife around the edge to prevent it from sticking to the sides of the pan. Allow the cake to cool completely in the pan on a wire rack, then refrigerate for at least 2 hours before serving. Serve cold with Whipped Coconut Cream.

At Kelly's Bake Shoppe, we make our own egg replacer for baking: sift ¾ cup tapioca starch with ¼ cup arrowroot starch. Store at room temperature in a clean glass jar with a screw-top lid. Anytime we need an egg, we just add 3 tablespoons of filtered water to 1 tablespoon of egg replacer and *voil*a!

DELECTABLE DONUTS (photo on page ii)

These donuts are so delicious and, even better, they're baked not fried. You'll need a donut pan, but it's worth buying one so you can whip up a batch of donuts whenever you like. Or whenever your friends and family clamor for them! When the donuts are cool, dip them in the topping of your choice—we've given you four options here, to keep everyone happy.

Active time: 20 minutes

Total time: 40 to 45 minutes

Makes 24 donuts

3 cups gluten-free all-purpose flour

1 ½ teaspoons baking soda

1 ½ teaspoons baking powder

1 teaspoon sea salt

¾ teaspoon xanthan gum

2 cups vanilla coconut milk yogurt

1 tablespoon fresh lemon juice

½ cup coconut milk

1 tablespoon arrowroot starch

¾ cup vegan shortening

1 ½ cups organic cane sugar

1 tablespoon vanilla extract

2 cups Chocolate Ganache (page 192)

    or 2 cups Vanilla Glaze (page 194)

    or 2 cups Strawberry Glaze (page 194)

    or cinnamon sugar, for dusting

1. Preheat the oven to 350°F. Lightly grease four donut pans (or use the same pan four times).

2. In a medium bowl, whisk together the flour, baking soda, baking powder, salt and xanthan gum. Set aside.

3. In a small bowl, combine the yogurt and lemon juice. Set aside.

4. In another small bowl, combine the coconut milk and arrowroot starch. Set aside.

5. In a large bowl and using an electric hand mixer, or in a stand mixer fitted with the paddle attachment, cream the shortening, then add the arrowroot mixture, sugar and vanilla. Beat for about 2 minutes, or until light and fluffy.

6. Add the flour mixture to the shortening mixture in three batches, alternating with the yogurt and beginning and ending with the flour mixture.

7. Scoop the batter into the prepared pan and smooth level with a knife. Bake on the center rack for 16 to 18 minutes, rotating the pan after 8 minutes.

8. Let the donuts cool completely in the pan before frosting. Dip the donuts one at time in the frosting of your choice, or dust with cinnamon sugar for a spicy change.

Cookies

PEANUT BUTTER PROTEIN COOKIES

We decided to pump up the protein power of these crunchy cookies by adding chia seeds and vanilla protein powder. Kapow! This is a great snack for that pesky afternoon energy slump. When you use all-natural nut butters, you're getting a good dose of healthy fats, too.

Active time: 15 minutes

Total time: 30 to 35 minutes

Makes 24 cookies

1 tablespoon ground flax seed

1 cup organic peanut butter or
    raw almond butter

2 tablespoons coconut oil, melted

2 tablespoons maple syrup

1 ¼ cups gluten-free rolled oats

½ cup coconut sugar or Sucanat

3 tablespoons vanilla protein powder

2 tablespoons chia seeds

2 teaspoons baking soda

½ teaspoon sea salt

½ cup vegan chocolate chips (optional)

1. Preheat the oven to 350°F. Line 2 large baking sheets with parchment paper.

2. In a small bowl, combine the ground flax seed with 3 tablespoons of filtered water and set aside to thicken.

3. In a large bowl, combine the peanut butter, coconut oil and maple syrup.

4. In medium bowl, whisk together the oats, coconut sugar, protein powder, chia seeds, baking soda and salt.

5. Add the oat mixture to the peanut butter mixture and stir well. Add the flax mixture and stir to blend. Fold in chocolate chips (if using).

6. Form the dough into 1-inch balls and place, about 2 inches apart, on the prepared baking sheets.

7. Bake for 8 to 10 minutes, or until edges are golden brown. Allow the cookies to cool completely on the baking sheets before transferring them to wire racks to cool completely.

These cookies will spread during baking. They also bake quickly, so check them after 8 minutes. If they aren't done, set the timer for another minute or two. The cookies will look soft when you take them out of the oven but they firm up quickly.

GOLDILOCKS OATMEAL-RAISIN COOKIES (photo on page 206)

The three bears might have forgiven Goldilocks if she had whipped up a batch of these cookies instead of gobbling up their porridge. This is a crisp, oat cookie that really benefits from the addition of chewy raisins, coconut shreds or chocolate chips. Go all out and try adding some dried goji berries to the mix!

Active time: 15 minutes

Total time: 25 to 30 minutes

Makes 24 cookies (enough for 12 people or 3 bears)

2 tablespoons ground flax seed

1 ½ cups Sucanat

¾ cup vegan butter

¼ cup organic cane sugar

1 teaspoon vanilla extract

1 ½ cups gluten-free all-purpose flour

1 teaspoon ground cinnamon

1 teaspoon baking soda

1 teaspoon xanthan gum

½ teaspoon sea salt

2 cups gluten-free rolled oats

1 cup raisins

½ cup unsweetened shredded coconut
  or ¼ cup vegan chocolate chips

1. Preheat the oven to 350°F. Line 2 large baking sheets with parchment paper.

2. In a small bowl, combine the ground flax seed with 6 tablespoons of filtered water and set aside to thicken.

3. In a large bowl and using an electric hand mixer, or in a stand mixer fitted with the paddle attachment, beat together the Sucanat, butter, sugar, and vanilla.

4. In a medium bowl, whisk together the flour, cinnamon, baking soda, xantham gum and salt. Add to the butter mixture, stirring together until smooth. Mix in the oats, raisins and coconut or chocolate chips until just combined. The dough will be a little dry but that is okay.

5. Form the dough into 1-inch balls and place, 2 to 3 inches apart, on the prepared baking sheets.

6. Bake for 12 minutes, or until cookie edges are golden brown. Allow to cool on wire racks. The cookies will keep in an airtight container for up to 10 days.

DID YOU KNOW?

Oats used to be considered unsuitable for celiacs until studies proved otherwise. Many commercial oats are cross-contaminated with wheat, barley or rye during harvesting, transportation, milling, processing and packaging. Use certified gluten-free oats.

WORLD PEACE COOKIE

This is the famous cookie we first created at the café as a nutritious and satisfying post-workout snack. We now bake these at Kelly's Bake Shoppe, and they sell out every day. Great for breakfast, snacks or any time you want a nutrition-packed treat.

Active time: 15 minutes
Total time: 30 to 35 minutes
Makes 30 cookies

1 cup plus 2 tablespoons gluten-free
    rolled oats

1 cup gluten-free all-purpose flour

½ cup organic cane sugar or coconut sugar

½ cup raw sunflower seeds

½ cup raw pumpkin seeds

¼ cup unsweetened shredded coconut

2 tablespoons ground flax seed

½ tablespoon ground cinnamon

1 teaspoon baking soda

1 teaspoon sea salt

¼ teaspoon xanthan gum

6 tablespoons coconut or canola oil

¼ cup coconut milk

2 tablespoons blackstrap molasses

2 tablespoons agave syrup

¾ cup vegan chocolate chips

⅓ cup raisins

1. Preheat the oven to 350°F. Line 2 large baking sheets with parchment paper.
2. In a large bowl, combine the oats, flour, sugar, sunflower seeds, pumpkin seeds, shredded coconut, ground flax seed, cinnamon, baking soda, salt and xanthan gum.
3. In a medium bowl, combine the oil, coconut milk, molasses and agave syrup.
4. Add the molasses mixture to the dry ingredients and stir. Fold in the chocolate chips and raisins, and stir until well combined.
5. Form the dough into 30 balls and place, about 1 inch apart, on the prepared baking sheets. Press each ball with the palm of your hand to flatten slightly.
6. Bake for 12 to 14 minutes, or until the edges are golden and the cookies are golden brown. Allow to cool slightly on wire racks.
7. Serve warm with a glass of unsweetened almond milk. Yum!

GINGER-CHOCOLATE COOKIES

These cookies offer the best of both worlds, with the ginger and chocolate combining to make a warming, soothing match made in heaven. The secret ingredient here is the fresh ginger added along with the ground ginger. It contributes surprising heat to offset the sweet.

Active time: 15 minutes
Total time: 25 to 30 minutes
Makes 24 cookies

1 tablespoon chia seeds

1 cup coconut sugar

¼ cup molasses

¼ cup canned pumpkin purée

¼ cup canola oil

2 cups gluten-free all-purpose flour

¼ cup cocoa powder

1 teaspoon grated fresh ginger

2 teaspoons ground ginger

½ cup crystalized ginger, chopped

1 teaspoon baking soda

1 teaspoon ground cinnamon

½ teaspoon xanthan gum

¼ teaspoon ground cloves

¼ teaspoon sea salt

¾ cup vegan chocolate chips

½ cup organic cane sugar

1. Preheat the oven to 350°F. Line 2 large baking sheets with parchment paper.

2. In a small bowl, combine the chia seeds with 3 tablespoons of filtered water and set aside to thicken.

3. In a large bowl, beat the chia mixture with 1 cup of the coconut sugar, the molasses, pumpkin purée and oil to form a thick mixture.

4. In a medium bowl, whisk together the flour, cocoa powder, fresh ginger, ground ginger, crystalized ginger, baking soda, cinnamon, xanthan gum, cloves and salt.

5. Add the dry ingredients to the wet ingredients and stir well. Fold in the chocolate chips. The dough will be stiff; don't worry!

6. Form the dough into 1-inch balls and roll them in the organic cane sugar. Place the dough balls, about 1 inch apart, on the prepared baking sheets and flatten each slightly with the palm of your hand.

7. Bake for 10 to 12 minutes, or until cookie edges are golden brown. Allow to cool on wire racks.

The unbaked dough can be frozen for up to 3 months.

CHOCOLATE CHIP COOKIES

This is another classic recipe that's improved by the addition of plant-based ingredients instead of dairy and eggs. Coconut oil provides a subtle natural sweetness and a wonderfully rich feel when you take a bite. And it's hard to beat the versatility of this recipe. Use whatever flour you have on hand: oat, sorghum or quinoa flours will all work well with the gluten-free all-purpose flour.

Active time: 18 minutes
Total time: 38 to 40 minutes
Makes 22 to 24 cookies

2 tablespoons ground flax seed

1 cup gluten-free all-purpose flour

½ cup oat flour

½ cup sorghum flour

1 teaspoon baking soda

½ teaspoon xanthan gum

¼ teaspoon sea salt

1 ¼ cups Sucanat

⅔ cup melted coconut oil

¼ cup organic cane sugar

2 tablespoons vegan butter

2 teaspoons vanilla extract

1 cup vegan chocolate chips

1. Preheat the oven to 350°F. Line 2 large baking sheets with parchment paper.
2. In a small bowl, combine the ground flax seed with 6 tablespoons of filtered water and set aside to thicken.
3. In a medium bowl, whisk together the all-purpose flour, oat flour, sorghum flour, baking soda, xanthan gum and salt.
4. In a large bowl, beat together the Sucanat, coconut oil, sugar and vegan butter until smooth. Beat in flax mixture and vanilla until smooth and creamy.
5. Add the flour mixture to the coconut oil mixture, stirring until just combined. Fold in the chocolate chips.
6. Drop heaping teaspoons of the cookie dough, about 2 inches apart, onto the prepared baking sheets.
7. Bake for 9 to 11 minutes, or until the edges turn golden brown. (For chewy cookies, bake for just 9 minutes.)
8. Allow the cookies to cool on the baking sheets for about 10 minutes before transferring them to wire racks to cool completely.

If you want your cookies to rise instead of baking up flat and chewy, chill the dough for 30 minutes before forming and baking the cookies.

CHOCOLATE RADICALS

These cookies are deliciously rich and loaded with chocolate flavor. We added one of our favorite snacks—gluten-free pretzels—for fun, and the salt and crunch really enhance the crazy-good factor of this cookie.

Active time: 20 to 25 minutes
Total time: 35 minutes
Makes 12 cookies

2 tablespoons ground flax seed

2 tablespoons chia seeds

1 teaspoon espresso powder

1 cup gluten-free all-purpose flour

2 ½ teaspoons baking powder

¼ teaspoon sea salt

¼ teaspoon xanthan gum

2 ½ cups vegan chocolate chips

6 tablespoons vegan butter

1 cup Sucanat

⅔ cup organic cane sugar

2 ½ teaspoons vanilla extract

1 cup raw pumpkin seeds

1 cup crushed, gluten-free pretzels

1 cup puffed quinoa cereal

½ cup chopped raw almonds

1. Preheat the oven to 350°F. Line a large baking sheet with parchment paper.

2. In a small bowl, combine the ground flax seed and chia seeds with ½ cup plus 2 tablespoons of filtered water and set aside to thicken.

3. In another small bowl, reconstitute the espresso powder with 2 tablespoons of boiling filtered water.

4. In a third small bowl, whisk together the flour, baking powder, salt and xanthan gum.

5. In a double boiler set over low heat, melt 2 cups of the chocolate chips with the vegan butter until smooth.

6. Remove from the heat and add the flax and chia mixture, dissolved espresso, Sucanat, sugar and vanilla, and mix well with a wooden spoon. Stir in the flour mixture.

7. Stir in the pumpkin seeds, pretzels, puffed quinoa, almonds and the remaining ½ cup of chocolate chips.

8. Form the cookie dough into 1-inch balls and place them, about 2 inches apart, on the prepared baking sheet. Press down lightly with the palm of your hand. They spread a lot so be sure to give them lots of room.

9. Bake for 10 to 12 minutes, or until the edges are crispy and the center is softer. If you overbake them, they will be crisp; if you underbake them, they will be chewy. Allow to cool on wire racks.

These cookies store well in the freezer.

CHOCOLATE-ALMOND BITES

These delicious frozen bites are unbaked, super simple and taste like cookie dough! The good news is that you can enjoy them as an anytime snack without guilt. We've even helped out with portion control. Conventional cookie doughs are loaded with unhealthy animal fats and full of processed white sugar. Not these!

Active time: 20 minutes

Total time: 1 ½ hours

Makes 12 to 14 bites

¾ cup gluten-free rolled oats

¾ cup almond flour, plus additional
    flour as needed

½ cup raw almond butter

5 tablespoons coconut oil, melted

4 tablespoons vegan chocolate chips

3 tablespoons maple syrup

2 tablespoons chopped raw almonds

2 tablespoons coconut sugar

2 tablespoons unsweetened
    shredded coconut

1 teaspoon maca powder

1 teaspoon hemp seeds

1 teaspoon vanilla extract

¼ teaspoon sea salt

1. In a food processor or blender, pulse the oats until they have a light floury texture.

2. In a large bowl, combine the powdered oats, ¾ cup almond flour, the almond butter, coconut oil, chocolate chips, maple syrup, almonds, coconut sugar, shredded coconut, maca powder, hemp seeds, vanilla and salt. The dough should be a little sticky. If it is too dry, add a little filtered water and stir again until it comes together.

3. Place the dough on a cookie sheet in the freezer for 5 minutes to firm up. If the dough is still too sticky, add a light dusting of additional almond flour.

4. With barely wet or lightly greased hands, shape the dough into small balls. Place on a large plate or cookie sheet lined with parchment paper and return to the freezer. Freeze for at least 1 hour or until firm.

STUFFED SNICKERDOODLES

Cookie sandwiches are one of our biggest sellers at the Bake Shoppe. You would think that cupcakes would be the most popular, but these little guys are so incredible, we have customers who drive for three hours just to indulge in them! In this recipe we've added a little dab of jam for some extra love.

Active time: 20 minutes

Total time: 2 ½ hours

Makes 15 cookie sandwiches

3 cups gluten-free all-purpose flour

1 ½ teaspoons xanthan gum

1 teaspoon baking soda

1 teaspoon sea salt

2 ¼ cups organic cane sugar

1 cup vegan butter

2 teaspoons vanilla extract

3 tablespoons ground flax seed

2 teaspoons ground cinnamon

Vanilla Buttercream Frosting (page 188)

1 cup raspberry or your favorite jam

1. Preheat the oven to 350°F. Lightly grease 2 large baking sheets.

2. In a medium bowl, whisk together the flour, xanthan gum, baking soda and salt.

3. In a large bowl and using an electric hand mixer, or in a stand mixer fitted with the paddle attachment, cream 2 cups of the sugar, the butter, vanilla, ground flax seed and 4 tablespoons of filtered water.

4. Add the flour mixture to the creamed butter and sugar. Mix until fully incorporated. Make sure no creamy mixture is left at the bottom and the dough is uniform throughout.

5. Form the cookie dough into two cylinders and wrap each tightly in plastic wrap. Refrigerate for 2 hours.

6. In a small bowl, combine the remaining sugar and cinnamon.

7. Form the chilled dough into 30 walnut-size balls. Roll each ball in the cinnamon sugar and place 15 balls on each prepared baking sheet. Allow the balls to come to room temperature. Using a fork, flatten each ball to ¼-inch thickness, making a crisscross pattern on the top of each with the tines of the fork.

8. Bake for 10 minutes, or until crispy on the outside but still chewy inside.

9. Allow the cookies to cool completely on wire racks. Spread the bottom of half of the cookies with the vanilla buttercream frosting. Spread the tops of the remaining cookies with raspberry jam.

10. Sandwich the cookies together, matching the frosting sides with the jam sides. Chill for 1 hour to firm up. Enjoy with a nice glass of Vanilla Almond Milk (page 26).

LEMON MELTAWAYS

These light and fluffy cookies are a perfect addition to your spring dessert table, or afternoon tea if you're feeling fancy. The chia seeds give this cookie a really nice crunch. And the other ingredients provide lemony melt-in-your-mouth goodness. This is a great cookie to make with kids; they love rolling the little balls in sugar.

Active time: 20 to 25 minutes

Total time: 40 to 50 minutes

Makes 24 small cookies

¾ cup organic cane sugar

⅓ cup vegan butter

⅓ cup coconut oil, softened

⅓ cup vanilla coconut milk yogurt or vanilla almond milk yogurt

3 tablespoons lemon zest

5 tablespoons fresh lemon juice

2 teaspoons vanilla extract

2 teaspoons natural lemon extract

1 teaspoon white chia seeds

2 cups gluten-free all-purpose flour

1 tablespoons arrowroot starch

2 teaspoons baking powder

1 teaspoon baking soda

1 teaspoon xanthan gum

1 teaspoon sea salt

⅛ teaspoon ground turmeric

1. Preheat the oven to 350°F. Line 2 large baking sheets with parchment paper.

2. In a large bowl and using an electric hand mixer, cream ½ cup of the sugar, the vegan butter and coconut oil for 3 minutes, or until smooth. Mix in the yogurt, lemon zest and juice, vanilla, lemon extract and chia seeds.

3. In a medium bowl, whisk together the flour, arrowroot starch, baking powder, baking soda, xanthan gum, salt and turmeric.

4. Add the flour mixture to the lemon mixture and combine well.

5. Form the dough into 1-inch balls. Roll the balls in the remaining sugar and place them about 1 inch apart on the prepared baking sheets. Flatten each ball slightly with the palm of your hand.

6. Bake for 10 to 12 minutes, or until the edges of the cookies are starting to brown. Allow the cookies to cool for 15 minutes on the baking sheets before transferring them to wire racks to cool completely.

Pumpkin Breakfast Muffins (page 177)

Muffins & Scones

PUMPKIN BREAKFAST MUFFINS

♥ Perfect for the morning or as a mid-afternoon on-the-go snack, these muffins were an original café recipe from way back in 2010! We add our own homemade granola to the batter for a yummy crunch and nutritious boost.

Active time: 25 minutes
Total time: 50 to 60 minutes
Makes 12 muffins

Nonstick cooking spray (optional)

2 tablespoons ground flax seed

¾ cup Sucanat

⅔ cup gluten-free all-purpose flour

⅔ cup sorghum flour

⅔ cup arrowroot starch

½ cup coconut sugar

2 teaspoons baking soda

1 ½ teaspoons ground cinnamon

1 teaspoon baking powder

¾ teaspoon xanthan gum

½ teaspoon sea salt

¼ teaspoon ground nutmeg

¼ teaspoon ground allspice

1 cup canned pumpkin purée

½ cup canola oil

1 cup Simply Delicious Granola (page 39)

½ cup raw pumpkin seeds

½ cup chopped walnuts

½ cup vegan chocolate chips (optional)

¼ cup raisins

¼ cup unsweetened shredded coconut (optional)

2 tablespoons hemp seeds

FOR THE GRANOLA TOPPING:

½ cup Simply Delicious Granola (page 39)

½ cup raw pumpkin seeds

½ cup coconut sugar

1. Preheat the oven to 350°F. Lightly spray a 12-cup muffin pan with cooking spray or line it with paper liners.

2. In a small bowl, combine the ground flax seed with 6 tablespoons of filtered water and set aside to thicken.

3. In a large bowl, whisk together the Sucanat, all-purpose flour, sorghum flour, arrowroot starch, coconut sugar, baking soda, cinnamon, baking powder, xanthan gum, salt, nutmeg and allspice.

4. In a medium bowl, thoroughly mix together the flax mixture, pumpkin purée, canola oil and ½ cup of hot filtered water.

5. Pour the wet ingredients into the dry ingredients. With a wooden spoon, mix until just combined.

6. Fold in the granola, pumpkin seeds, walnuts, chocolate chips (if using), raisins, coconut and hemp seeds.

7. Using an ice-cream scoop, divide the batter among the muffin cups, filling them to within ½ inch from the top.

8. To make the granola topping, combine the granola, pumpkin seeds and coconut sugar in a small bowl. Sprinkle the mixture over the muffins, dividing evenly.

9. Bake for 25 to 30 minutes, or until a cake tester inserted in the center of a muffin comes out clean. Allow to cool in the pan for about 15 minutes, then transfer to wire racks. Best served warm.

These will keep well in the freezer
if they're individually wrapped.
Allow 1 hour to defrost before eating.

BLUEBERRY OAT MUFFINS

Who doesn't love blueberry muffins? These tasty little guys are one of our favorites at home and in the Bake Shoppe. It's important to use wild blueberries for these. In fact, you should choose wild blueberries whenever possible because they have more than double the antioxidants of commercially farmed blueberries, and more flavor. So go wild!

Active time: 30 minutes
Total time: 55 to 60 minutes
Makes 12 muffins

Nonstick cooking spray (optional)

2 tablespoons ground flax seed

1 cup almond or coconut milk

1 cup gluten-free rolled oats

1 ¼ cups gluten-free all-purpose flour

¼ cup sorghum flour

¼ cup arrowroot starch

2 teaspoons baking powder

1 teaspoon ground cinnamon

½ teaspoon baking soda

½ teaspoon xanthan gum

¼ teaspoon sea salt

¾ cup coconut sugar or Sucanat

¼ cup palm shortening

2 tablespoons maple syrup

2 teaspoons vanilla extract

¾ cup fresh or frozen wild blueberries
    (see sidebar)

FOR THE CRUMBLE TOPPING:

4 tablespoons gluten-free rolled oats

3 tablespoons coconut sugar

2 tablespoons vegan butter

1 teaspoon ground cinnamon

1. Preheat the oven to 350°F. Lightly spray a 12-cup muffin pan with cooking spray or line it with paper liners.
2. In a small bowl, combine the ground flax seed with 6 tablespoons of filtered water and set aside to thicken.
3. In a small saucepan, warm the milk to a simmer, then add the oats. Turn off the heat and let the oats soak for 20 minutes.
4. In a large bowl, whisk together the all-purpose flour, sorghum flour, arrowroot starch, baking powder, cinnamon, baking soda, xanthan gum and salt.
5. In a medium bowl and using an electric hand mixer, beat the coconut sugar, shortening, maple syrup and vanilla until smooth. Stir in the oat-milk mixture and the flax mixture.
6. Add the oat mixture to the flour mixture, combining the ingredients by hand to keep the batter tender. Fold in the blueberries with a wooden spoon.
7. Using an ice-cream scoop, divide the batter among the muffin cups.
8. To make the crumble topping, combine the oats, coconut sugar, butter and cinnamon in a small bowl. Sprinkle the mixture over the muffins, dividing evenly.
9. Bake for 22–24 minutes or until a cake tester inserted in the center of a muffin comes out clean. Let the muffins cool completely on a wire rack before serving.

If you use frozen blueberries for these muffins, increase the baking time by 3 minutes.

ROASTED APPLE MUFFINS

These muffins become really special if you get creative and roast two or more different types of apple. Granny Smith, Pink Lady or good old Canadian McIntosh—just use whatever looks best to you. It doesn't matter if the apples have different textures or levels of sweetness, as that will make the muffins even more interesting.

Active time: 15 minutes
Total time: 90 minutes
Makes 12 muffins

FOR THE ROASTED APPLES:

2 cups cored, peeled and chopped apples

½ cup Sucanat

¼ cup fresh lemon juice

1 teaspoon ground cinnamon

¼ teaspoon ground nutmeg

¼ teaspoon ground allspice

FOR THE MUFFINS:

2 cups gluten-free all-purpose flour

2 tablespoons ground cinnamon

2 teaspoons baking powder

1 teaspoon baking soda

1 teaspoon sea salt

¾ teaspoon xanthan gum

¼ teaspoon ground allspice

¼ teaspoon ground nutmeg

⅔ cup Sucanat

⅔ cup coconut milk or rice milk

½ cup canola oil

⅓ cup applesauce

1 teaspoon vanilla extract

1. Preheat the oven to 350°F. Line a baking sheet with parchment paper, and lightly spray a 12-cup muffin pan with cooking spray or line it with paper liners.

2. To make the roasted apples, toss together the apples, Sucanat, lemon juice, cinnamon, nutmeg and allspice in a medium bowl. Spread the apple mixture over the baking sheet. Bake for 30 minutes, rotating the baking sheet halfway through. The apples will be soft. Let the apples cool on the baking sheet.

3. To make the muffins, whisk together the flour, cinnamon, baking powder, baking soda, salt, xanthan gum, allspice and nutmeg in a medium bowl.

4. In another bowl, combine the Sucanat, coconut milk, oil, applesauce and vanilla and stir well. Add to the dry ingredients and stir until the batter is smooth. Stir in the cooled, roasted apples.

5. Using an ice-cream scoop, spoon about ⅓ cup of the muffin batter into each muffin cup. Bake for 20 minutes, or until a tester inserted into the center of a muffin comes out clean. Allow to cool on a wire rack before serving.

LEMON, ORANGE & CRANBERRY SCONES

These scones are perfect for a summer Sunday brunch. We love the sour pucker you get when you eat a really lemony treat and for that, the lemon needs to be abundant. Here the orange zest emphasizes the taste of the lemon, making these scones a citrus sensation.

Active time: 20 to 25 minutes
Total time: 40 to 45 minutes
Makes 8 scones

1 tablespoon ground flax seed

2 cups gluten-free all-purpose flour

⅓ cup plus 1 tablespoon organic cane sugar

2 tablespoons Sucanat or coconut sugar

2 tablespoons finely grated orange zest

1 tablespoon baking powder

2 tablespoons finely grated lemon zest

1 teaspoon baking soda

½ teaspoon sea salt

½ teaspoon xanthan gum

½ cup vegan shortening, chilled

½ cup vanilla coconut milk yogurt

2 tablespoons fresh lemon juice

2 teaspoons vanilla extract

1 teaspoon natural lemon extract

¾ cup dried cranberries

1 tablespoon rice milk

½ cup Lemon Glaze (page 194)

1. Preheat the oven to 350°F. Line an 8-inch round cake pan with parchment paper.

2. In a small bowl, combine the ground flax seed with 3 tablespoons of filtered water and set aside to thicken.

3. In a large bowl, whisk together the flour, ⅓ cup sugar, Sucanat, orange zest, baking powder, lemon zest, baking soda, salt and xanthan gum.

4. Add the shortening and cut it in with a fork or a pastry cutter until the mixture is crumbly and resembles coarse oatmeal.

5. In a small bowl, whisk together the flax mixture, yogurt, lemon juice, vanilla and lemon extract.

6. Add the yogurt mixture to the flour mixture and stir well. You may need to mix with your hands; this dough will be heavy and sticky. Gently fold in the cranberries, trying to distribute them evenly.

7. With lightly greased hands, pat the dough into the prepared cake pan, flattening and shaping the dough into a smooth, flat round. Brush the top with the rice milk and sprinkle with the remaining 1 tablespoon sugar.

8. Bake for 18 to 20 minutes, or until firm and light golden brown. Allow to cool on a wire rack, then cut into 8 wedges and drizzle with lemon glaze.

PUMPKIN-SPICE SCONES

Can you tell we love pumpkin? This combination of fall flavors will make you want to go out and jump for joy in a pile of leaves! Earthy, warming and rich, these scones aren't too sweet: they're just right.

Active time: 15 minutes

Total time: 35 to 40 minutes

Makes 8 scones

2 tablespoons ground flax seed

1 cup sorghum flour

½ cup gluten-free all-purpose flour

½ cup tapioca starch or potato starch

5 tablespoons Sucanat

1 tablespoon baking powder

1 teaspoon xanthan gum

1 teaspoon ground cinnamon,
     plus extra for sprinkling

½ teaspoon sea salt

¼ teaspoon ground cloves

¼ teaspoon ground nutmeg

7 tablespoons vegan shortening, chilled and
     cut into small pieces

½ cup canned pumpkin purée

3 tablespoons maple syrup

3 tablespoons molasses

3 tablespoons rice milk

¼ teaspoon apple cider vinegar

1 cup Maple Nutmeg Frosting (page 191)

Cinnamon, for sprinkling

1. Preheat the oven to 350°F. Lightly grease a 9-inch pie dish or round cake pan.

2. In a small bowl, combine the ground flax seed with 6 tablespoons of filtered water and set aside to thicken.

3. In a large bowl, whisk together the sorghum flour, all-purpose flour, tapioca starch, 4 tablespoons of the Sucanat, baking powder, xanthan gum, cinnamon, salt, cloves and nutmeg.

4. Add the shortening and cut it in with a fork or a pastry cutter until the mixture is crumbly and resembles coarse oatmeal.

5. Add the flax mixture, pumpkin purée, maple syrup, molasses, rice milk and vinegar. Beat briefly until the dough is just mixed and has formed a smooth mass. Don't overbeat or your scones will be tough.

6. With lightly greased hands, pat the dough into the prepared cake pan, flattening and shaping the dough into a smooth, flat round. Sprinkle the top with the remaining Sucanat.

7. Bake for about 20 minutes, or until the scones are firm and light golden brown. Allow to cool on a wire rack, then cut into 8 wedges. Ice with maple nutmeg frosting, and serve with a sprinkling of cinnamon on top.

RASPBERRY SCONES

This is a lovely wake-up treat on a Sunday morning. Imagine the aroma of fresh raspberries as they're baking . . . Perfect in August when they are in season. We love these with our Strawberry Frosting (page 190).

(page 190)

Active time: 15 minutes

Total time: 30 to 35 minutes

Makes 8 scones

1 ½ cups gluten-free all-purpose flour

½ cup white rice flour

1 tablespoon baking powder

½ teaspoon xanthan gum

½ teaspoon sea salt

½ cup plus 1 teaspoon organic cane sugar

⅓ cup coconut oil

1 tablespoon finely grated lemon zest

1 tablespoon vanilla extract

1 cup fresh raspberries, plus a few extra
   for serving

1 teaspoon rice milk

1 cup Strawberry Frosting (page 190)

1. Preheat the oven to 350°F. Line a 9-inch round cake pan with parchment paper.

2. In a medium bowl, whisk together the all-purpose flour, rice flour, baking powder, xanthan gum and salt.

3. Add the ½ cup of sugar, coconut oil, lemon zest and vanilla. Stir until a thick, slightly dry batter is formed.

4. Slowly pour 1 cup of hot filtered water into the batter and mix thoroughly. Using a rubber spatula, gently fold in the raspberries, just until they are marbled throughout.

5. With lightly greased hands, pat the dough into the prepared cake pan, flattening and shaping the dough into a smooth, flat round. Brush the top with the rice milk and sprinkle with the 1 teaspoon of sugar.

6. Bake for 15 to 18 minutes, or until a cake tester inserted in the center comes out clean.

7. Allow to cool in the pan for 15 minutes. Transfer the scones to a wire rack to cool completely, then cut into 8 wedges. Ice with strawberry frosting, and top with fresh raspberries.

Frostings, Fillings & Sauces

VANILLA BUTTERCREAM FROSTING

Active time: 10 minutes

Total time: 10 minutes

*Makes enough to frost 24–36 cupcakes
or one 8-inch triple-layer cake*

1 cup palm shortening, room temperature

¼ cup vegan butter, softened

4 ½ cups powdered sugar, sifted

2 tablespoons vanilla extract

2 tablespoons almond or rice milk (optional)

1. In a large bowl and using an electric hand mixer, or in a stand mixer fitted with the paddle attachment, blend the palm shortening with the vegan butter for about 5 minutes, or until smooth and fluffy.

2. Slowly add the powdered sugar, ½ cup at a time, and continue to blend until the sugar has been completely incorporated. Add the vanilla and beat well.

3. If the frosting is too stiff, add the almond milk, 1 teaspoon at a time, until the buttercream is the desired consistency. If you add too much milk and the buttercream is too soft, sprinkle in another tablespoon of powdered sugar.

To color the frosting a beautiful pink color,
add ½ teaspoon of beet juice with the vanilla extract in step 2.

CHOCOLATE BUTTERCREAM FROSTING

Active time: 10 minutes

Total time: 10 minutes

*Makes enough to frost 24–36 cupcakes
or one 8-inch triple-layer cake*

1 cup palm shortening, room temperature

¼ cup vegan butter, softened

3 ½ cups powdered sugar, sifted

¾ cup raw cacao powder, sifted

2 tablespoons vanilla extract

2 tablespoons almond or rice milk

1. In a large bowl and using an electric hand mixer, or in a stand mixer fitted with the paddle attachment, blend the palm shortening with the vegan butter for about 5 minutes, or until smooth and fluffy.

2. Slowly add the powdered sugar, ½ cup at a time, and continue to blend until the sugar has been completely incorporated.

3. Blend in the cacao powder, in three additions, until it is well incorporated. Add the vanilla and beat well.

4. Add the almond milk, 1 teaspoon at a time, until the buttercream is the desired consistency. (Adding milk by the teaspoon ensures the frosting won't get too runny and will stay fluffy.)

CREAM CHEESE FROSTING

Active time: 10 minutes

Total time: 10 minutes

*Makes enough to frost 18 cupcakes
or one 9-inch double-layer cake*

1 ½ cups vegan cream cheese

1 cup palm shortening, room temperature

2 tablespoons maple syrup

2 tablespoons vanilla extract

Pinch of sea salt

6 ½ cups powdered sugar, sifted

½ cup unsweetened shredded coconut
    (optional)

1. In a large bowl and using an electric hand mixer, or in a stand mixer fitted with the paddle attachment, blend the vegan cream cheese and palm shortening until smooth.
2. Add the maple syrup, vanilla and salt. Mix until combined.
3. Slowly add the powdered sugar, ½ cup at a time, mixing after each addition and scraping down the sides of the mixer as necessary. Mix on high speed for 2 to 3 minutes, or until the frosting reaches the desired consistency.
4. Stir in shredded coconut (if using). Refrigerate in a sealed container until ready to use.

STRAWBERRY FROSTING

Active time: 10 minutes

Total time: 30 to 40 minutes

*Makes enough to frost 18 cupcakes
or one 9-inch double-layer cake*

1 cup fresh or frozen strawberries

½ cup vegan butter, softened

½ cup palm shortening , room temperature

4 cups powdered sugar, sifted

1 teaspoon vanilla extract

Almond or rice milk as needed

1. In a blender or a food processor fitted with the metal blade, purée the strawberries until smooth.
2. Transfer the strawberry purée to a small saucepan and simmer for 20 to 30 minutes, or until the volume has reduced by half. Remove from the heat and set aside to cool.
3. In a medium bowl and using an electric hand mixer, beat the vegan butter with the palm shortening until whipped and smooth. Slowly add the powdered sugar, ½ cup at a time, and continue to blend until the sugar is fully incorporated. Add the vanilla and beat well.
4. Add the cooled puréed strawberries and gently blend until uniformly pink throughout. If the frosting is too stiff, add a little almond milk.

MAPLE NUTMEG FROSTING

Active time: 10 minutes

Total time: 10 minutes

Makes 1 cup, enough for 8 scones

⅓ cup palm shortening, room temperature

2 tablespoons vegan butter, softened

1 ½ cups powdered sugar, sifted

2 tablespoons maple syrup

1 tablespoon rice milk or coconut milk

2 teaspoons vanilla extract

Pinch nutmeg

1. In a large bowl and using an electric hand mixer, blend the palm shortening and vegan butter for about 5 minutes until light and fluffy.
2. Slowly add the powdered sugar, ½ cup at a time, and continue to blend until the sugar is fully incorporated, scraping down the sides of the mixer as necessary.
3. Add the maple syrup, milk, vanilla and nutmeg and continue to blend on high speed until the frosting reaches the desired consistency. Be careful to use just a pinch of nutmeg as the taste can be overpowering.

CHOCOLATE AVOCADO FROSTING

This frosting is good for you! It's raw, vegan and even fits with the Paleo Diet. Make sure you give the avocados a gentle squeeze to ensure they are perfectly ripe before you use them. Underripe avocados will not blend in properly and won't yield the luscious texture you want. This frosting works on almost anything, and is just perfect on our Mexican Cupcakes (page 133).

Active time: 10 minutes

Total time: 10 minutes

Makes enough to frost 18 cupcakes or one 9-inch double-layer cake

4 ripe avocados, pitted (see sidebar)

1 ½ cups maple syrup

1 cup raw cacao powder, sifted

¼ teaspoon sea salt

1. In a blender, combine the avocados with the maple syrup until smooth.
2. Slowly add the cacao powder, in three batches, scraping down the sides of the blender as necessary. Add the salt and blend once more.
3. Use the frosting right away or, for a firmer frosting, refrigerate it for 15 minutes.

An easy way to peel and pit an avocado is to slice it in half around the pit, then twist the two halves to separate them. Scoop out the pit, then use a large spoon to scoop out each avocado half.

CHOCOLATE GANACHE

This is one of our favorite recipes at the Bake Shoppe. It's simple and versatile and we use it to fill our cupcakes and top our award-winning brownies. It's important to use warm water in the mix to get the satiny shine that's so enticing.

Active time: 5 minutes
Total time: 5 minutes
Makes 2 cups

1 ½ cups powdered sugar, sifted

⅔ cup cocoa powder, sifted

2 tablespoons melted palm shortening
    or vegan butter

1. In a medium bowl, mix the powdered sugar and cocoa powder with the melted palm shortening and ⅓ cup of warm filtered water until thoroughly combined.

2. If the ganache is too stiff, add a little more filtered water. If it's too runny, add a little more sugar.

LEMON CURD

This is perfect as a filling for a banana cupcake or between the layers of a lemon cake. We also love to use this to make dainty cookie sandwiches with our Lemon Meltaways (page 173).

Active time: 12 to 15 minutes
Total time: 3 ½ hours, including refrigerating time
Makes about 1 ½ cups

4 tablespoons arrowroot starch

1 ¼ cups organic cane sugar

2 tablespoons finely grated lemon zest

½ cup fresh lemon juice

1 ½ cups coconut milk or soy milk

2 tablespoons vegan butter

1. In a small bowl, dissolve the arrowroot starch in 3 tablespoons cold filtered water.

2. In a small saucepan, combine the sugar, lemon zest and juice. Cook over medium heat, whisking constantly, until the sugar has dissolved.

3. Add the arrowroot starch mixture and the coconut milk and continue whisking gently for 6 to 8 minutes, or until the mixture begins to thicken and bubble. Remove from the heat when the mixture reaches pudding-like consistency. Stir in the vegan butter.

4. Pour the lemon curd into a glass storage container and cover with plastic wrap, ensuring that the wrap makes full contact with the surface of the curd. Allow to cool completely, then refrigerate for at least 3 hours before using.

SALTED CARAMEL SAUCE

We love our caramel sauce! This sauce has won us dozens of awards over the years. It's especially good on Chocolate-Pumpkin Bread Pudding (page 115). Who doesn't love warm caramel sauce on ooey-gooey pudding?!

Active time: 8 minutes
Total time: 8 minutes
Makes 1 ½ cups

3 tablespoons arrowroot starch

1 cup soy or coconut milk creamer

¾ cup Sucanat

½ cup brown rice syrup

1 tablespoon vanilla extract

¼ to ½ teaspoon sea salt

1. In a small bowl, dissolve the arrowroot in 3 tablespoons of the creamer.
2. In a small saucepan over medium heat, whisk together the remaining creamer, Sucanat, rice syrup and dissolved arrowroot starch. Whisk constantly for 5 minutes or until mixture has thickened.
3. Remove from the heat and whisk in the vanilla and salt to taste. Serve warm.

CARAMEL DRIZZLE

This is a key ingredient in our Banana Butterscotch Loaf (page 147). It is an easy, no-cook sauce that tastes great on just about anything you can think of!

Active time: 5 minutes
Total time: 5 minutes
Makes ½ cup

4 tablespoons Sucanat

1 tablespoon coconut oil

1 tablespoon vanilla coconut milk yogurt

1 teaspoon vanilla extract

¼ teaspoon sea salt

1. In a medium bowl and using an electric hand mixer, combine the Sucanat, coconut oil, yogurt, vanilla and salt for about 3 minutes or until the mixture emulsifies.
2. Use immediately or refrigerate for up to 1 week.

VANILLA GLAZE

This—and the strawberry variation below—works well with any of our scones and makes a great topping for our Delectable Donuts (page 154).

Active time: 10 minutes
Total time: 10 minutes
Makes 1 cup, enough for 8 scones or 12 donuts

1 cup powdered sugar, sifted
1 tablespoon rice milk or coconut milk
1 teaspoon vanilla extract

1. In a small bowl and using an electric hand mixer, beat the powdered sugar, milk and vanilla for 20 seconds or until the mixture is runny but not too thin.
2. If you're glazing scones, transfer the glaze to a small plastic bag. Clip off one corner and squeeze the bag to pipe a zigzag pattern of glaze on each scone.
3. If you're using it to glaze donuts, just dip the top of each donut in the glaze.

VARIATION:

Strawberry Glaze

For a delicious Strawberry Glaze, combine the following ingredients and proceed as above.

1 cup powdered sugar, sifted
1 teaspoon unsweetened rice milk or coconut milk
1 teaspoon beet juice
1 teaspoon strawberry jam
1 teaspoon vanilla extract

LEMON GLAZE

Sweetly tart, this glaze will make your mouth pucker. It's the simplest recipe but packs big, fresh flavor. We love the taste of lemon, especially when it's combined with raspberries, so try this on our Raspberry Scones (page 185).

Active time: 5 minutes
Total time: 5 minutes
Makes ½ cup

1 cup powdered sugar, sifted
4 teaspoons fresh lemon juice

1. In a small bowl, mix together the powdered sugar and the lemon juice until smooth.

RASPBERRY SAUCE

Fresh and healthy, and full of antioxidants, vibrant flavor and raw goodness, this is a beautiful sauce for your morning porridge, drizzled on a raspberry scone or as a flourish over a rich chocolate cake.

Active time: 5 minutes
Total time: 5 minutes
Makes 1 ½ cups

1 cup fresh or frozen raspberries

⅓ cup softened pitted dates

⅓ cup agave syrup or coconut syrup

2 teaspoons chia seeds

⅛ teaspoon sea salt

1. Place the raspberries, dates, agave syrup, chia seeds, salt and ¼ cup of warm filtered water in a blender. Blend for 1 minute or until the sauce is smooth.

2. Refrigerate any unused sauce in a sealed container for up to 5 days.

WHIPPED CASHEW CREAM

Dollop this on desserts, granola, pancakes, waffles, hot cocoa . . . the list goes on. Whenever you would use whipped cream, you can substitute whipped cashew cream. People are amazed by how delicious and rich this is. We think it tastes better than dairy.

Active time: 5 minutes
Total time: 4 ¾ hours
Makes 2 ¼ cups

1 cup raw cashews

¼ cup maple syrup

½ teaspoon vanilla extract

Pinch of sea salt

¾ cup coconut oil, melted

1. Put the cashews in a bowl and add enough cold filtered water to cover them. Cover the bowl and leave to soak for 30 minutes in the refrigerator. Drain and rinse.

2. In a blender, combine the cashews, maple syrup, vanilla and ¼ cup of filtered water until smooth.

3. Add the salt and, with the blender running on low speed, very slowly drizzle in the melted coconut oil. Increase the speed to high and blend until completely smooth and whipped.

4. Pour the whipped cashew cream into a storage container and chill for at least 4 hours or overnight before using.

WHIPPED COCONUT CREAM

This whipped cream is a staple in our kitchens because of its absolute simplicity and versatility. Enjoy it on its own, or add it to fresh fruit, crumbles, cakes, milkshakes or anything else—it's great on just about everything. The coconut milk has to be full-fat in order to yield a rich cream. The light stuff simply won't work!

Active time: 10 minutes

Total time: about 6 hours, including refrigerating time

Makes 1 cup

1 can (12 ounces) full-fat coconut milk

2 teaspoons maple syrup

1 teaspoon vanilla extract

1. Refrigerate the unopened can of coconut milk upright for at least 6 hours or overnight.

2. Place a glass or metal bowl in the freezer for at least 5 minutes to chill.

3. Remove the can of coconut milk from the fridge. Flip the can upside down and then open it. The coconut water and cream will have separated, leaving the cream at the bottom of the can. Drain off and reserve the coconut water (see sidebar), leaving the cream in the can.

4. Scoop the coconut cream into the prepared chilled bowl. Using an electric hand mixer, whip the coconut cream for 3 to 5 minutes, or until light and fluffy.

5. Mix in the maple syrup and vanilla. Serve immediately or refrigerate for up to a week.

You can keep the coconut water to use in smoothies, sauces or even salad dressings.

Acknowledgments

KELLY'S THANK YOUS:

This book has been burning inside me for a long time. I'm just so ecstatic that Erinn wanted to write it with me. Thank you my dear, sweet kid for being my partner in crime. This book is so incredible because of your tirelessly hard work. You've put up with so much from me; I would've fired me by now.

My husband Ken, the love of my life, you have been my comfort and my inspiration. Even in our chaotic lives you always made the time to hold me, or run me a hot bath, or make me dinner, or all of the above. Thank you for your patience as I took on yet another challenge. To my dying day, you will be deeply nestled in my heart. You are the frosting on my cupcake and President of my fan club.

Michael Rennie, my boy, the son I never had. You have been my friend for ten years now and it is still hard to grasp how lucky I am, and how lucky Erinn is, to have you. You are the most genuine soul I know and your words of encouragement helped in more ways than you will ever know.

Mom, you are the reason for my strength. You are a brilliant, selfless woman who taught me about the fire and drive within the feminine wisdom, and showed me the definition of class and tenacity. You are my superhero.

Shannon, my stoic sister. Thank you for giving me a soft shoulder and enabling my "controlled meltdowns." It was needed. You are my #BFF of fifty years now. I love you forever!

My nephew Connor, and my niece Alyssa. Both of you gave me the inspiration to plow ahead and make a difference when I saw what kids were eating, because it's just not food. These recipes are for you two rock stars, and all your friends.

Kathleen Riordon, our uber-talented superstar personal assistant—our "load her up with everything, never hear a bleep of a complaint, works tirelessly into the wee hours of the morning" girl—and Jessalynn Elliott, the "Erinn clone" and general manager extraordinaire of the Bake Shoppe. I am grateful for your integrity and work ethic. Without you two, we would not have had the time to create this book. Period.

Laurie Syer, our mother hen manager, who tends to our flock of girls and Andy. We are kindred spirits, Laurie, and I thank you for choosing to share your path with us. Jai Ganesha to the goddess within.

Carolyn Halls, my BFF since we were twelve years old, we don't even have to be together and yet we are. You got breast cancer and decided that food was going to heal you and it did. You are living proof of the power of good food. I am so proud of you. You have always cheered me on and I thank you for that blessing.

Elizabeth and Alan, our landlords that chose us. Thank you for believing in us!

Ella Bernhard, my lawyer and dear friend, who has my back always, even when I don't.

ERINN'S THANK YOUS:

Mom, for giving me life and for teaching me the true meaning of girl power. I love you!

Dad, for being an incredible and steady support in my life, and for taking me on trips to see the world when I was little. I love you so much.

Michael, for being my number one fan, supporter and beacon of light. Thank you for saying "I love you" back when we were fifteen years old.

Ken, my step-dad, for teaching me everything you know about being a successful entrepreneur. I'm so grateful for your love and guidance.

My grandparents, for loving me unconditionally. Poppa Russ, for instilling a strong sense of creativity, passion and curiosity into a five-year-old girl. I miss you so much.

Zoe, for being the best cat, my brilliant confidante, and such a great example of why people should adopt (and bring some zen into their life).

Lana Wilson, for teaching me to embrace my inner mermaid.

My 7th and 8th grade teacher, Kristin Vikse (Ms. V), for offering me nurturing support so I could flourish and reach for the stars.

Jessalynn and Kathleen, thank you for allowing us the space to write this book. Words can't even describe how grateful I am to have you both in my life.

To all animals, for all of the pain and suffering you endure as a result of our actions. I'm so sorry.

BIG THANK YOUS FROM BOTH OF US:

Our loyal fans and customers: This book is for you! Without your love and encouragement, your emails and comments and reviews, this book never would have happened. Thank you for coming into our lives.

Todd, Rony, Josh and Mel at Faduchi Group, your creative ideas, brand and graphics are simply incredible. Thank you!

Paul Fedorko, NYC agent extraordinaire (crush time!). Thank you dear, sweet, hunk of a man! None of this would exist if you had not seen something that needed to be published, persevered and pursued us. We love you!

Alison MacLean, where would we be without you? Still on page one. You showed us the ropes and how to forge on to book-writing nirvana. Your talent and skills as our editor have brought us joy every single day. We are eternally grateful.

Robert McCullough (crush time again!), thank you for signing us and for supporting these two newcomers. The tireless hours you have given to our book will be eternally acknowledged and most respected. We know we have been a royal pain in the ass but we hope we were worth it. With love, your sweets.

Lindsay Paterson, editor extraordinaire. We did it! Well . . . you did it and we became cultured in creating a cookbook. You are such a doll and a brilliant editor, and we are in awe of your talent, and your editing and multi-tasking skills. You polished our book into this vision of extraordinary loveliness and we are thrilled with the finished product.

Alyssa Wodabek and Chris Sue-Chu, thank you for making this book come to life with your incredible gift of photography! You two are an amazing team. You have captured the very essence of this book. Every image and detail is jaw-droppingly gorgeous. We're willing to bet you will be bombarded with calls to get you to work on other books. But too bad! We have you! Thank you for your hard work, long hours and re-shoots.

Joanne Tsakos, your food styling consistently blew us away, with the help of Lara Mcgraw, Catherine Doherty and Genevieve Wiseman's props—thank you! And Fiocca Studio, thank you for allowing us to use your spectacular space.

Our recipe testers at Kelly's Bake Shoppe: Laurie, Kathleen, Nicole, Rachel, Erin, and Jen—thank you for being our guinea pigs!

Chocolate Cake (page 102)

Index

Goldilocks Oatmeal-Raisin Cookies (page 159)